If You Vote, You Have No Right to Complain

by

John Everett

A list of this author's books is available at www.cakescorner.me.

If You Vote, You Have No Right to Complain

2016/10/20

Imagine that you made a bet with someone. It doesn't matter what the bet is over–it may be the outcome of a football game or the toss of the dice. But whichever game, and for whatever reason aside, you and a rival enter into a wager. The stakes are as follows: The loser's house will be burned to the ground. Now, assuming that you take the bet, you are aware that you are entering a wager where someone's house will be burned down. To such a bettor, the desired outcome is a house burning down. Of course, you will surely wish that it shan't be your house, but you will wish that *a* house burn down. You'll just wish it's the house of your rival. Notice I have said nothing of intentions or motives. Morally speaking, it does not matter why you are taking the bet. Maybe you need the winnings for emergency surgery or to make your car payment. But the reason does not matter. No matter what the outcome, someone's property will be destroyed for the benefit of a short-term gain by the winning party.

It is despicable to take a bet where you know that no matter what, someone's house will be destroyed. What would be more despicable still would be to delude yourself into thinking that your rival will be better off, and/or that the destruction of his house is either secretly benefiting him or the charred rubble is just an illusion. Of course, if you were the loser you would not fall for this assurance; you would recognize the lie for what it is and you would want your house back. If this situation seems absurd, it is only because I have substituted the words "house" and "wager" for "liberty" and "vote."

Did that seem hostile and absurd just for the sake of riling you up? Well, I like to have two purposes in my writing–riling up the reader is just the secondary one. If you carefully examine the above situation in the new context, you ought to find that it is accurate. When two rival voters enter their voting boxes, they want to impose their views and/or the views of their candidates onto each other. The loser suffers a reduction in liberty for the short-term gain of the winner. What is worse, each voter enters the booth knowing this. Each voter has as his goal the

2

trampling of liberty; he just hopes it will be his opponent's and not his own. But here is where the analogy breaks down. No bet-winner will assure the loser that the smoldering pile of ash that was once his house is to his benefit. But the voter, upon "winning" the election, will assure the loser that trampled liberties are to his own gain. This is the height of arrogance and self-aggrandizement. If I, the winner, voted for something, then it must mean that it is right and therefore the loser is blessed to have that something forced upon him. If I, the winner, want something, then that thing is good and the loser is blessed for being compelled to pay for it. Whether the winner is correct in saying that the "something" is good or not is irrelevant. For if that winner had lost the election, he would not be so well-assured that his loss was to his benefit, would he?

If you were to witness a house being swallowed by flames because of a bet, would you give much credence to the bitter and sorrowful complaints of the loser? I imagine you might say something like, "You entered this bet knowing that someone's house would burn down and now you're complaining because it was yours? You have no right to complain because you chose to legitimize this arrangement with your participation." If a person who never agreed to any bet suffered the loss of his house, however, then his complaint would be valid, yes? What if two persons made a bet and the third person's house was at stake? Then the third person would have every right to complain. Only a heartless beast would snidely retort, "If you didn't want to lose your house then you should have taken the bet. If you had won then your house would have been spared. If you don't bet then you have no right to complain." What cruel and callous inhumanity would lead a person to say such a terrible thing? Well, you ought to know if you've ever told someone, "If you don't vote then you have no right to complain." Pardon me, but isn't it the other way around? If you vote, knowing that someone's liberty shall be violated, then isn't it true that you surrender your right to complain the moment you cast your vote? You know that someone's house shall burn down; you're just hoping it won't be yours.

And now I imagine the intentions will come along. You "need" to take the bet so you can pay the bills. You "need" to take the bet because if you don't then someone else will. You "need" to vote because individuals are less adept at running their own lives than faceless bureaucrats a thousand miles away are. Yes, yes, of course. Intentions and excuses always nullify the immorality of an act, don't they? Unless, of course, they're the actions of your rivals. In that case, the actions are vile no matter what intentions the rivals may have. After all, what kind of monster would burn down someone's house because "the ash will make great fertilizer and the rebuilding process will create jobs?" What a psycho!

So what if person A votes to curtail the liberties of B and C, person B votes to curtail the liberties of A and C, and person C chooses to not vote because he would rather that no one's liberties be curtailed? I can tell you who's the least-likely to win in that election. And that's the real problem. If you choose to not take a bet, then the bettors cannot include you–they must bet only amongst themselves. But where voting is concerned, everyone must either be an aggressor or a victim. A sales representative at a car dealership may rest happily at night despite knowing that there are billions of persons who will never test drive one of his cars, but politicians and voters cannot tolerate the idea of someone trying to live outside their betting book. To live outside the circus freak show, to mind one's own business and have no interest in petty rivalries with one's fellow man: this is unthinkable! Even though C may be fine with the idea of bettors betting amongst themselves and leaving him alone, he will never have the same courtesy afforded him. He must be a spectator at the freak show whether he likes it or not.

Speaking of freak shows, the 2016 US election will come down to Donald Trump and Hilary Clinton. Most Americans who vote will be doing so for a variety of reasons: fear, spite, anger, and force of habit being among them. I am happy to say that I will not be voting. If someone's house shall burn down, I will not be one of the bettors. I will not give credence and legitimacy to the freak show. I certainly will not endorse Donald "Burn down their houses" Trump, Hilary "Burn down their houses" Clinton, or even Gary "Burn down a smaller building than a house; maybe just a shed or car port" Johnson. If I were to vote for a politician, I would be endorsing their actions. Which is worse: a lion mauling zoo patrons, or someone unlocking the lion's cage to let it out? I'm not worried about dictators. A dictator is only one person. It is voters who help dictators get into power and/or keep them there. If you endorse the actions of a politician for any reason, it is just as bad as committing the acts yourself–perhaps worse. I will not vote for any politician simply because I am not evil, and I do not wish to control the lives of my fellow human beings for any reason.

So when Hilary wins the election (edit: I wasn't expecting the Democratic Party's ploy to backfire that spectacularly.), don't blame me. Even if we operate on the faulty assumption that voting makes a difference, choosing between two politicians is akin to choosing between Beelzebub and Satan. But you must understand that when you vote, what you're actually doing is choosing yourself. You're not going to pick the politician whose platform drastically differs from yours, right? So you will vote for the politician who will force your beliefs (more or less) onto others. When Clinton becomes president she will force the beliefs of her voters onto hundreds of millions of persons who do not want them. If Trump or Johnson were somehow to become president, it would be the same situation. So when a voter casts a vote, they are really saying "I want my opinions to be forced onto my fellow human beings against their will." Or maybe they're just saying, "Clinton/Trump is bad, but at least they're not as bad as Trump/Clinton!" Either way, whoever wins, we'll lose.

But can voting ever be permissible? It can be if the vote is done defensively. The noted anarchist writer Lysander Spooner wrote that voting is OK if done defensively, meaning to vote in opposition to any and all new laws or regulations. In Nevada, for example, there are several new proposals on the ballot for 2016. One proposal would require gun purchasers to first submit to an additional background check. I will vote against this proposal because it would violate the liberty of all Nevadans. Another proposal asks whether we ought to continue placing an additional tax on gasoline to fund new roads. I will be voting against this one as well, because I do not believe it right to force Nevadans (or anyone) to surrender their hard-earned money in order to fund roads they may never even use. Besides, the Nevada government could save a lot of money by auctioning off roads (at least the minor ones) to private individuals, organizations, or companies. No state-funded maintenance would be required on these roads ever again and the current budget would be more than adequate to build new freeways and maintain current ones. Of course, that would mean less control and less power in the hands of the Carson City mafia—this, as I explained before, is unthinkable. But as for me, I will not endorse any such enterprise that shall control other persons' lives—no matter how good the intentions may be. I will vote only to oppose government, and when asked to vote for a person I will refuse. What course of action you take is up to you. You have your freedom, after all. Use it well. I will now leave you with the words of the late, great George Carlin:

"If you vote, you have no right to complain. People like to twist that around, I know. They say, 'Well, if you don't vote you have no right to complain,' but where's the logic in that? If you vote and you elect dishonest, incompetent people and they get into office and screw everything up, you are responsible for what they have done. You caused the problem. You voted them in. You have no right to complain. I, on the other hand, who did not vote, who in fact did not even leave the house on election day, am in no way responsible for what these people have done and have every right to complain as loud as I want about the mess that you created, that I had nothing to do with."

Strike at the Root: Understanding the Source of Problems in Our Society

2016 January

No one can deny that there are many problems facing us today. Poverty, illiteracy, corruption, and so on are enduring obstacles in our lives. Many people do their best to combat these problems, but in order to do this effectively we have to first figure out what is causing these problems. The trouble is, people can't seem to agree on the causes of most of these issues. It seems that everyone has different answers. Depending on the person you ask, you might hear the answers: because of the poor, because of immigrants, because of rich corporations, because of lobbying, because of corrupt politicians, and so on. What I would like to discuss now, however, is an answer that hasn't been very popular but is steadily gaining traction. There is a radical movement that puts forth the idea that government in general is the primary cause of most societal problems. Not a certain Government in particular, mind you. Not a Republican Government or a Democratic Government. Not a parliamentary or congressional Government. Just government in any of its myriad forms. Such a simplistic worldview suffers from a fundamental problem, and I want now to explain what it is.

Simply put, Government is not the problem. The problem is the evilness of the human heart. Ultimately, don't you agree that this is the root cause of societal problems? Crazy gunmen don't commit mass shootings because their hearts are filled with love. Bank executives don't foreclose on families' homes and take massive bailouts because they lack evil in their hearts. Specifically, it's the presence of evil inside of us that prevents the world from being a perfect place. But why can't government be a part of this evil presence? Well, let me explain.

Think about what government is. It's not a real, tangible thing, so how can we blame government? Sure, there are tangible things related to government. You can touch the wall of a capital building. You can read government documents or shake the hand of a senator, but those things *per se* are not government, just as a textbook or a chalkboard are not education. These things are merely implements. Government, no matter how you view it, is an imaginary concept; it exists only in our minds, no matter how many of its implements (charters, bureaus, offices, politicians, licenses and permits, etc.) may be real. Every government is the following idea: a group of persons who get together and manage the lives of their fellow human beings. The persons who do this are real, but their idea is imaginary. An apple is a real thing; it can be bitten into and tasted. The Capitol is a real thing; made of white stone and towering magnificently over the capital city. But government itself is just a name given to the agreements reached by specific men and women, and perhaps the documents they record these agreements on. The government is only reified in our imaginations. Every government action is just an action carried out by a group of persons who are called leaders or rulers. Every government action, then, begins inside someone's heart. This is an important step toward understanding how the bad things around us can happen. If persons who want to do evil end up in positions of power, they can abuse their authority and do bad things that have far-reaching effects. But it's not government itself that is responsible since it's not a tangible thing. It's the persons who commit evils. Now, if a person did something evil for just a moment and then disavowed it, the world would not be in such a bad shape; the primary thing that allows for the perpetuation of evil is the art of making excuses.

People in general are very skilled at making excuses. This is caused by cognitive dissonance (the discomfort that comes from having one's beliefs challenged) and confirmation bias (the tendency of humans to reject whichever facts oppose our beliefs and accept whichever lies confirm our beliefs). Deep down inside, we know when our actions are wrong, but most people, most of the time, choose to justify our actions so they seem right. We want to be right, but not at the expense of adjusting our behavior. And so if you read something that goes against your beliefs, your first instinct will be to dismiss it, or say, "But! But!…" and try to refute it. Everyone does this. Depending on the person and the belief being challenged, cognitive dissonance can lead a person to do downright crazy things in order to preserve their beliefs at all costs. Cognitive dissonance can result in anger, frustration, desperation, name-calling, and so on, all in an effort to preserve what we believe.

Have you ever noticed that certain people are passionately fighting for something you oppose? Let's say, for example, that you abhor fracking (hydraulic fracturing) and want to ban or regulate it, but then there are others who love it and fight to keep fracking operations going. Why would they do this, do you think? They certainly don't think they're in the wrong. But here's the thing: If they are in the wrong but they don't know it, it's probably because of their bias. They won't stop fighting for what they believe, because their bias encourages them to keep their beliefs instead of changing. Because of this bias you'll be hard pressed not to find an abundance of excuses for bad behavior. People will say "But! But!..." and follow this with a million different excuses. "But! I don't think it's a good idea!" "But! It's a matter of public safety." "Those things are bad for you." "Not in my back yard." "Think of the children!"

Every bad action will have plenty of its own excuses. Because confirmation bias is emotionally charged, these excuses will often be paired with attacks on the opponent. "You must hate the poor!" "Oh, so you want us to get killed?" "You just don't care!" "It's obvious that you're just ignorant." "Nazi!" What these excuses and attacks say is irrelevant. All that matters is that they **are** excuses and attacks. All that matters is that they attempt to turn evil into good. It is simply an attempt to replace the truth with one's beliefs. Most of us love our beliefs more than we love the truth. Using these justifications is a great way to silence opponents. I'm sure many German citizens in the 1930s were told, "You just don't care about Germany then! I guess you want these inferior peoples to destroy us!" That attack is based on emotion; facts are not dependent on emotions.

When justifications enter the picture, pointing out the wickedness of a deed cannot deter the resolve of the doer. At that point s/he is convinced that the evil deed has become right. When a bunch of persons get together to form a mob, then this bias will only be magnified, and each person in that mob will not feel personally responsible for actions they commit while in the mob. This is why persons cannot be deterred by the bad effects of a public policy. They are hiding in the mob and judging the policy by its intentions rather than judging it based on its results. Because they believe in the action, they believe in it

9

despite whatever ills may come. If they judged it by its results and saw that the results are bad, then they would feel compelled to change their beliefs and stop supporting that policy. Persons want to defend their beliefs at the expense of everything else.

Let us examine, for example, the so-called "war on drugs." Now, if you support the war on drugs, then this paragraph may prove my point that humans care more about their beliefs than the truth. Read on if you dare. There are certain chemical substances called drugs, which a lot of people like to use, but many others consider these substances a threat and want to prohibit their consumption by law. Now, I previously explained that the true problem in the world is the wickedness of the human heart. Drugs can never be a problem because they have no will of their own, nor any sin nature. They can only be abused by those with sin inside their hearts. If drugs were to vanish from existence tomorrow it would not mitigate the problem at all. Humans would still have sin in our hearts and we would find other things to abuse. Most persons don't understand this concept, however, and delude themselves into thinking that prohibiting drugs will make the problem better. They focus on the tool for committing evil rather than focusing on the evil itself. So they decide to abuse power; they get together in a government and try to forcibly control the lives of their fellow humans. They say "Don't exercise your free will when it contradicts our wishes, or else you shall be punished." This policy is just as evil as the desire to harm one's own body with drugs. Actually, the prohibition is more evil. Whereas the consumption of drugs hurts one's body, enforcing prohibition harms someone else's body by kidnapping them with handcuffs and throwing them in jail; and it also harms the souls of those who enforce or support the policy. It is not spiritually healthy at all to know that you morally support the kidnapping and imprisonment of men or women whose only **actual** crime was minding their own business.

If you look at the war on drugs from any angle you will see that it has had only negative effects. It has resulted in a disproportionately high rate of incarceration for poor black and Hispanic Americans. It has funded countless drug cartels and brought violence to previously peaceful cities. There have been many other negative results, but pointing these out will have no effect on those who support the war on

10

drugs. They only care about the war's good intentions, and not its bad results.

And this is where the aforementioned excuses come in. Supporters of the war will invariably make up justifications for their mass kidnappings. "Drugs are bad for you (so it's OK to snatch you from your home and throw you in a cage)." "I don't want my children to be around junkies (so I would rather them grow up in a police state)." "Drug prohibition is for your own good because drugs are bad for you (but getting shanked in prison is much better)." As I explained before, what these excuses say is irrelevant. What is important is their underlying meaning: "I believe it's OK for me to force my will upon others, and I know deep down that it's wrong so I'm choosing to justify it however I can." This is not to say, of course, that supporters of a certain policy are automatically monsters. I know that they have good intentions–everyone does. There is not a single person of sound mind who wakes up and says, "I want to make the world a worse place today." Everyone has good intentions and believes that their crusade is the moral one. But good intentions do not nullify bad actions. And if we understood this, we would be critical of our actions. But it all goes back to the original problem: the human heart is deceitful above all things. We choose to believe we can make the world a better place by controlling the lives of others, without realizing that the desire for power **is** a major part of the problem. We would realize that our good intentions aren't really good if we criticized our beliefs but, again, we want to change reality instead of changing our beliefs. The desire to control the lives of others comes about as a direct result of wishing to twist around reality. The belief that prohibition (or mandating) will make the world a better place stems from: 1. the assumption that one's beliefs are true and 2. that the ends justify the means. God created the world according to His will and it was good originally, so if we re-create the world according to our will, it'll be good again, right?

The problem with this way of thinking is that we are not God. God wants the world to be good but allows us to make our own decisions; humans who have a thirst for power are not so gracious. If someone does something you don't like or abstains from something you like, then you probably believe it's a good thing to control them or

11

punish them. And because humans realize deep down inside that this is wrong, they attempt to further justify these actions by proxy. If a bunch of other persons (lawmakers) gets together and forms a government, and a bunch of other persons (police) enforces the policies, then it stops being wrong. This, of course, is a lie. If it is wrong for a man to kidnap another, then it is wrong for a thousand men to kidnap a thousand others. Because the imaginary machine of "government" is hidden under many, many layers of proxy, however, most of us never even stop to think about or question it.

No one of sound mind would think it right to hold a gun to a man's head and say, "I want you to do ___ or else I'll punish you." But that same person will happily pay someone to put on a uniform with a badge and hold the gun in his behalf. Once this happens then that man will feel separate from his actions by proxy. Even the police officer will feel separate from his actions because there are many layers of proxy to punishment as well. If someone breaks a law, the punishment will not usually be a gun to the head right away. We have devised many other decrees such as fines, sub poenas, censures, gag orders, community service, incarceration, etc. Punishment is suggested by officers but upheld by judges, oftentimes in collaboration with juries. Together, they carry out these progressions of punishment as needs be. But should all of the previous steps fail, you must realize that eventually a gun will be used to control the "offending" party. Think about the progression. If you break a law, you'll be fined. If you refuse to pay the fine, you'll have a lien or hold placed on your property. If you refuse to comply, your property will be stolen. If you defend your property, you will be kidnapped. If you resist being kidnapped and defend yourself with a weapon, you will be shot. Eventually, every single policy, every single law and regulation, every single "government" decree, is backed by the threat of violence. Most citizens would just pay the fine and avoid being shot, obviously, but that's not my point. ***Eventually*, every law is backed by violence or the threat of violence**. And thus comes about a great dilemma. No matter how good your intentions, no matter how many excuses you have, no matter how much you want to change the world for the better, any "government" action you support is backed by the threat of violence and forcibly imposed on you and your fellow humans. If that seems moral to you, then you have my pity.

And now come more excuses. "But the government is protecting you!" "But it's not immoral when we have democracy!" "That's the price you have to pay to live in a free society!" "If you don't like it then leave!" "Think of the CHILDREN!" Or perhaps you fully agree with the notion that "government" action is violence, but you just don't care. If you think that, I'm afraid there's nothing I can say to you. But if you believe that "government" action is not inherently violent, then I have this to ask. At what point does an act transition from immoral to moral? If it's immoral to impose one's will onto others, then at what point does it cease to be immoral? If it's immoral to rob a rich man, then how is it moral to tax a rich man? (I'll wait for you to finish spewing out excuses and justifications like an obnoxious drunk spewing vomit.) Think of this for a while and I'm sure that you'll come to the conclusion that the two actions are entirely different because they have two different names. Taxing and robbing are two different words, so they must be two different actions. This is another layer of proxy, though. Taxation is the act of compelling a man (by threat of violence) to surrender a portion of his property so it can be spent by someone else. The only difference between this and robbery is a matter of size. Robbery is perpetrated by one man against another; taxation is perpetrated by millions against millions more. Of course, no one defends the honor of the robber or makes up excuses for him. Because of the aforementioned magnifying effect (really just a type of proxy), the excuses of millions of persons in a mob are stronger than the excuses of one person. Everyone else is doing it; we're all paying taxes together; think of the children; we never personally demand the money from our victims–only by proxy. If the fellows with suits decree a tax and the fellows with badges enforce it, then the act stops being immoral. Such an attitude has led to untold atrocities.

Let us return to the war on drugs. If ordinary humans break into a man's house to steal his property, that is called "breaking and entering" and "theft." If those ordinary humans are wearing costumes with badges and handcuffs, however, then it becomes a "no-knock raid." If a husband tells his wife that she cannot drive the car without his permission or else he'll extort money or throw her in a cage, that is called "domestic abuse." But if that husband is sitting behind a desk at the DMV, then it's called "drivers' licensing." I guarantee you that everything an abusive spouse may do, participants of "government" do to a far greater degree. But because we call things by different names, we believe that we are no longer held morally accountable for our actions. And here come more excuses. "But having a driver's license is a matter of public safety!" "I don't want to drive on the road along with unlicensed maniacs!" "THINK OF THE CHILDREN!!!" Because there's no way auto manufacturers could be in charge of licensing in a way that's based on voluntary exchange instead of violence, right? (You will eventually discover that every excuse and justification you come up with defending "government" will be not only factually wrong, but morally wrong as well.) Also, you skipped right over the point of what I was saying. You may agree with me, with a smug sense of self-righteousness, that enforcing drug prohibition is immoral, but as soon as I replace "war on drugs" with any policy you support, your smug little smirk will fall right off your face. Dressing up your language doesn't change the nature of the actions that those words represent. "Government" can't be a problem because it's just a word masking violence behind proxy. Electing officials to impose your agenda onto others is no better than imposing your agenda onto others yourself, and in fact is worse. The robber does not pretend that he has your best interests at heart or that he will spend your money for your benefit better than you could if you had kept it.

When God asked Adam why he ate the fruit, Adam passed the blame onto Eve so that he would be innocent by proxy. When God asked Eve why she ate the fruit, she passed the blame onto the devil so that she would be innocent by proxy. And all this time later, we are still doing the same thing. Nazis at the Nuremburg trials said, "I was just following orders." Rather than taking responsibility for our actions, we are passing the blame onto others and passing our responsibility onto others. But it's a lie. You are responsible for your actions and your beliefs. Even though you haven't ever busted down an innocent man's door to kidnap him for smoking a plant, you are still responsible if you morally support it. Time for another excuse. "I don't support police brutality either! We just need to elect the right official who can fight corruption!" You miss the point entirely, dear reader. For one thing, if your system has to have the right person in office to work, then it's a horrible system. Second, the problem isn't who's in office. As I've said several times before, the problem is the wickedness of the human heart. It's not the wickedness of Bob or Steve or Cindy or Jennifer that's the

14

problem. Everyone has such wickedness. You can't make the world a better place through violence because violence itself is negative. It doesn't matter if someone is a "good" ruler and uses violence slightly less than the other guy, or uses violence to achieve what you want instead of what "they" want. **It would just be violence for a cause you like**. If you disagree with this sentiment then it's because you believe an act ceases to be violent if it's carried out for your agenda. You, then, are no different from a robber, a scam artist, or a despot.

Even if you don't support the war on drugs, there is *something* tyrants do that you support. Maybe you support corporate subsidies, bailouts, censorship, the income tax, a monopoly on fiat currency, medicare, socialized medicine, a standing army, gun control, a minimum wage, the deportation of immigrants, the EPA, etc. But there is ultimately no difference between the violence behind the war on drugs and the violence behind any other "government" action. If you would not hold a gun to the head of a business owner and demand that he hire a certain percentage of female employees, then you should not support the idea of someone in a magical costume with a badge doing it in your behalf. But everyone likes bias until it differs from their own.

Do you understand what I am saying? There is no such thing as government; there is only a group of persons who, compelled by confirmation bias, carry out various agendas by proxy. We place our faith in them because we want to believe that they are demi-gods who can bring about utopia by forcing others to go along with their plans. That is the fault of each individual who chooses to believe it. You cannot blame democrats or republicans; only individual human beings are to blame for their deceit. Government is not the problem (since it doesn't exist); it's a symptom of the problem. The belief that violence is a good thing is a symptom of the problem. The problem, really, is the belief that we are gods and we know best.

So how can you fix the problem? The first answer is to get your own house in order. Stop thirsting for power. Stop desiring to control other persons' lives. It's an odd mixture of narcissism and cynicism that compels a person to prescribe government as a remedy. You believe that humans are too stupid/evil/etc. to run their own lives, but are

15

smart/virtuous enough to elect *other* stupid/evil humans to run their lives for them. If you want the world to change, then be the change you wish to see. Instead of asking, "Without government, who would (_____)?" If you do it, then it shall be done. I don't have to wonder how persons can be educated without government. I never have to wonder if private education is possible because I'm living proof that it is. I educate others every chance I get. I've given free music lessons, driving lessons, Latin and Japanese tutoring, etc. without being forced to at gunpoint. I'm not saying this to brag about my accomplishments–I'm saying it to prove a point. The kind of person who actively makes the world a better place is the kind of person who has no reason to put his faith in an imaginary entity run by corrupt psychopaths and supported by millions of bloodthirsty worshipers. If you see a problem in the world and your first instinct is to solve it at gunpoint, then you are sorely deceived.

More excuses? What is it this time? "But government needs to step in and fix things caused by freedom!" "There's no way private charity can be active enough to solve these problems!" "We need government help to fill in the gaps." "We need government to maintain peace and order!." "We need to make the selfish people help too!" "**THINK OF THE *CHIIIIIILDREEEEEN*!!!!!**" There is great irony in the proclamation that "selfish people should do what I want." The desire to make others do what you want is selfish. Aside from that, there is no doubt that problems will exist without violent policies, but that can never be eradicated. The real problem, remember, is the wickedness of the human heart. Utopia can never be brought about because there is still sin. I do not deny that a world without "government" would still be rife with sin and shortcomings. But the threat of violence, in and of itself, is a sin and shortcoming. The question is: would you rather live in a world of shortcomings with violent psychopaths controlling your life, or a world of shortcomings without them? That's like asking, "Would you rather be hungry *with* a nail driven through your head, or hungry *without* a nail driven through your head?" The absence of "government" is no guarantee that some men won't murder, but the presence of "government" is a guarantee that some men will. Consider that 8 Million private murders were carried out in the 20th century, compared to well over 200 Million state-sanctioned murders. Does that sound orderly and peaceful to you? We have been taught to think that anarchy is chaos, but it's really the belief in "government" that is chaos.

If you dislike Coca Cola you are more than welcome to stop drinking it; but if you dislike Adolf Hitler or Che Guevara you cannot simply say "No thanks," and continue to live your life in peace. You will be shot. If you dislike George Bush or Barack Obama you cannot simply say, "No thanks," or else you will go to jail for breaking some "law" or another. There was a man named Irwin Schiff who refused to pay income taxes. He didn't like being robbed by the IRS on a regular basis, so he said, "No thanks." In 2015, he died of old age in prison. Being forced to do what others tell you to is the price you have to pay to live in a "free" society. If you don't like a bodyguard you can fire him. If you don't like police brutality, you still have to fund them with your paycheck or else they'll kidnap you.

The idea of jailing someone for tax evasion is proof that rulers are neither logical nor compassionate. In order to punish Mr. Schiff for not giving them money, they spent millions of tax dollars to keep him locked in a cage, where he couldn't earn any money to pay taxes. Putting someone in jail for dodging taxes results in a net loss for the state. This is proof that it's not about good sense or public order. It's about control. It's about power, and striking fear into the hearts of the people by making an example out of a rebel. It's no different from the mafia breaking the kneecaps of a delinquent debtor.

Now that you have run out of excuses for the time being (I hope), please use the opportunity to examine your beliefs and challenge them. You have been lied to your whole life, and trying to escape that indoctrination is very difficult. You have been taught that freedom constantly produces disastrous results and that our lord and savior Government must step in to save the day. You were told that Lincoln went to war to free the slaves, FDR ended the great depression, and Obama kept the peace in the Middle East. (Read Tom Woods' book The Politically Incorrect Guide to US History to see how wrong your teachers were.) Such lies are so deeply ingrained in our minds that they can persist for years. I speak this from personal experience, having been a centrist democrat and before that a republican (sort of). Curiously, the war on drugs was my last great ideological holdout after having renounced my worship of government. I supported it simply on the basis

17

that drugs are bad for you. What I eventually learned is that the belief in government is far worse than any drug. I still abstain from drug use, having never indulged once in my life; opposing the war on drugs does not mean that I want everyone to be addicted to drugs. All it means is that I do not wish to force my ideas onto others. I now apply this to every law and policy.

If you do not hold the same position, let me ask you: Which of your rights would you like to have a democratically elected official violate? Would you like to have a law passed saying that you can't use a cell phone past 6:00 p.m.? Would you like it if that leader passed a law prohibiting you from wearing jeans for no reason, or a law requiring you to purchase and carry a gun, as well as purchasing a minimum amount of ammunition and attending mandatory gun-care classes? If you think that government is good, then tell me which hypothetical law, violating *your* rights, you would support. If you can't answer then you must realize that you only support government because you want to force YOUR ideas on others, not the other way around. Sure, you would gladly pay taxes to fund a program that you support, but if you had to pay the same amount of tax money on a program that you diametrically oppose, you would not be happy. Trying to end a program would be very difficult. If you don't like automobiles you are more than welcome to spend your money on a bicycle or spend no money and walk. But if you want to stop funding a government program then you had better hope that your "representatives" agree with you. In the meantime you'll still have to pay for the program you hate; otherwise you'll be kidnapped, just like Irwin Schiff.

And that brings me back to the main point. "Government" isn't the problem. It's only a symptom of the thirst for power. The true problem lies within the hearts and minds of men and women who want to enslave their fellow humans (I'll explain this in the next section). The only way to limit this thirst is to learn love for God. If you love God, you will love your fellow man. If you love your fellow man, you will no longer wish to enslave them. If everyone on Earth suddenly stopped wishing to enslave each other, the world would be a dramatically better place, even with every other problem or symptom remaining. If you wish to see a world like that, stop loving yourself more than you love God. Be educated and educate others. Love others. Bring change into the world yourself instead of electing thieves and liars to try and do it for you. Do unto others as you would have them do unto you. Above all, challenge your own beliefs as much as you challenge others'. If you challenged your own beliefs even half as much as you challenged others' then you would be a whole lot better off for it. The truth matters a whole lot more than your petty opinions.

I'm sure that I ruffled a few feathers when I stated that taxation is no different from robbery and can be equated to slavery. We have been conditioned to think that "we" have a right to other persons' tax money. If rich people or corporations use loopholes to lessen their tax burden, most Americans feel that they stole from "us." Somehow, protecting your money from theft makes you a thief. I can sympathize with this thought process, though. Bombs are expensive and the rich should pay their fair share. Those Middle Eastern children won't blow up themselves, you know. We need all the tax money we can get.

Anyway, if you disagree that taxation is slavery (but refer to persons who voluntary work at a company as "wage slaves") then please walk me through your mind for a minute. I'll present you with a hypothetical scenario and I'd like you to tell me what you think. All right, here we go.

- Scenario 1

A man named George is living on a plantation in the American South, circa 1850. He doesn't want to live there, but he's forced to. George must get up early every day and pick cotton for his master. George must pick cotton or else he will be punished. Usually this punishment is getting whipped, but if he adamantly refuses to comply, he may be tied down or shot. He may only live on the plantation in a specially designated house that his family had to build themselves. Only after a hard day's work can George go home to tend to his own needs. The cotton that he picked will be sold by his master, who will keep 100% of the money.

Do you think George is a slave? Well, I should certainly hope so. The main characteristics of his life are as follows:

- He must live and work where the government tells him.
- He must relinquish 100% of his property.
- He must comply with all demands made of him or he will be punished.
- He does not have recognized sovereignty–the master may kill him (but not vice versa).

These are all hallmarks of slavery. You might want to add that the work George must do is very hard and this was another hallmark of slavery, but this work was actually quite light compared to the work slaves did in Brazil during the 18th and 19th centuries, or Poles during the 20th century German occupation. Slaves in the US were unique because they lived long enough to breed. Most Brazilian slaves died within five years of being imported from Africa because the work and environment were lethally difficult. So back-breaking work isn't necessarily a condition of slavery, right? Someone could bring up the case that if George were truly a slave, he'd already be dead. I hope you disagree with that, because it'll come in handy for scenario 2.

- Scenario 2

George's master notices that the North is far more industrialized than the South, and much richer. The master likes the sound of this, so he decides to change George's lot. He figures that if he sets George to more profitable work than cotton, the whole plantation will be richer for it. So now George's work is quite different. Now George can choose his own workplace and place of residence as long as it is inside the town where the master and his friends live. In order that George should be motivated to earn more money, he is allowed to retain up to 70% of his earnings- the master only keeps 30% for himself. But in order to squeeze money out of George through more subtle means, the master requires George to commute to work in a specific way. If George wants to walk, it must only be in designated paths. If he wants to ride a carriage, he must buy a letter of passage from his master, allowing him to ride without being whipped. Of course, in order to keep George in line, a taskmaster continues to follow him about with whip at the ready. If George breaks one of his master's many arbitrary whims, he will be punished. He may be whipped, or have an additional portion of his 70%

earnings confiscated, or so on. George's master uses some of the ill-gotten gains to build a church next to his plantation. The church was paid for with money that was taken from George. Whether George chooses to attend that church or not, he paid for it anyway. George must remain a subject of his master for all his life; for he can only leave on his master's own terms. The master may set his price of freedom at an astronomically high price, or have George captured if he stops paying the 30% fee after leaving for another master.

The characteristics of George's life are now thus:

- He may choose where to work and live, as long as it is inside boundaries set by his master.
- He is allowed to keep up to 70% of his earnings before fees and fines.
- He may freely use the church that the master built next to the plantation.
- He does not have to crawl to work; he may walk or ride in a carriage as long as he follows his master's rules and pays whatever fees are levied for the privilege.
- As long as George follows the rules and keeps quiet, he will probably never be whipped.

Is George still a slave? His lot in life is much more luxurious than it was previously. Just as the slave in Brazil would wish to work on the plantation, so would every plantation slave wish he were George. But is George still a slave? He no longer has to relinquish 100% of his earnings to his master, so we must ask, "At what percentage does the seizure of earnings cease to be slavery?" Yes, George may keep up to 70% of his earnings, but his everyday life is still dictated by the whims of a greedy and cruel master. He will still be whipped by the taskmaster if he disobeys and he must still do what his master says, whether on the plantation or off. Furthermore, he knows that it is the seizure of his own earnings that pays for the taskmaster's watchful gaze. Yet if he were to complain, a fellow "free" slave would rebuke him for not appreciating what he has, and for scoffing at the church that the benevolent master built for him. Now let's look at the final scenario.

- Scenario 3

George is transported to the 21st century where his master no longer lives in a plantation house. His master now works from within a marble dome in the capital city. There is a 40% chance that George will be forced to purchase a license for his job. He must also purchase a license if he wishes to run his own business. George is free as long as the government regulates his every action. He must buy a license in order to get married, cut down a tree on his own land, go fishing, breed dogs, or any number of other things. George must every day contend with the frustration of being told what he can or cannot eat, consume, say, buy, sell, rent, lease, or create. Any inventive idea that George comes up with must be subjected to a lengthy and expensive review by an uncaring bureaucracy. Any money that George saves will invariably start to diminish in value over time because of inflation. Although George is constantly reassured that he is a free man, he must continue to pay up to and exceeding 30% of his earnings to his master. Refusal to do so will result in George being threatened with additional fees or being caged. The men who would cage George will be paid from money that the masters took from George's paychecks. George knows that because of well-intentioned government policies, his chances of being caged are very high as a young, black male.

If George wishes to leave the US, he must do so according to the whims of his masters. They will charge around $4,000 to start the process for revoking citizenship, and even after George moved to another country he would still have to pay his American masters a percentage of his income–all while being subjected to the whims of his new masters also. George knows that at every moment a minion of his masters is spying on him, reading all of his communications and watching his every move. His masters could, at any moment, have him killed by raining down death from the sky and there is nothing he or his family could do about it. His sovereignty as a being is not recognized, but the sovereignty of his masters is. Although George can choose where to live and where to work (within certain boundaries, both physical and imaginary), he knows that he is very much a slave. He still picks the cotton at his masters' discretion and they keep however much they want. Whenever George complains, a more loyal slave rebukes him, defending the masters that oppress them both. An ingenious system has arisen, in which government indoctrination camps begin to brainwash children as young as five years old; by the time these children are eighteen, they are lifelong drones of the state. Of course, the funding for these camps comes from George's paychecks, whether he wants to enroll his children in them or not.

Now tell me, what's the difference between George and you? The main difference is that you are much more likely to think that you are free. You have been taught to believe that because you're allowed to vote, that you can be an active participant in the democratic process. The government isn't really oppressing you; they're just looking out for your best interests. Sure, the government messes up, but it's far better than having freedom. If you don't like it you can always work within the system to change it, because a corrupt system can easily be used to fight corruption, right? You are told again and again, "You are free. Now do as I say." If Johann Wolfgang von Goethe was correct when he said, "None are more hopelessly enslaved than those who falsely believe they are free," then patriots are much more slaves than the slaves ever were.

The all-encompassing definition of slavery is the infringement upon the freedom of association. All freedom is, invariably, freedom of association. If someone is protecting your freedom of speech, it means that you are able to, without punishment, associate with whichever ideas or thoughts you wish. If no one is encroaching upon a person's freedom to own property, then it means that a person is allowed to be associated with whichever property he wishes. And every true freedom also includes its opposite. If you are free to do something, you are also free to abstain from it. After all, if you choose to drink milk, then at that moment you are simultaneously associating with milk and disassociating with wine. If you are free to speak, you are free to remain silent, for the freedom of association with speech necessarily includes the freedom of disassociation with speech. Every freedom on Earth is in essence the freedom of association, and every freedom must also include its own opposite. Slavery is really just the infringement by one party on the freedom of association of another. George was a slave because he was forced to associate with the plantation, forced to associate with its master, forced to disassociate from the fruits of his labor and the reward thereof. Anyone who is forced to associate with the US and its constitution is likewise a slave. If you are free as an

American citizen, then you are equally free to be a non-citizen without penalty or pain. To say, "You signed a social contract at birth and now you owe America your allegiance and tax dollars," is no different from telling a slave that he signed a social contract by being born on a plantation. I never signed any such contract, and I never will. I never signed the Constitution or any other law. I never told Congress to be my representatives, and I never told police to be my taskmasters. If a contract may be forced upon a person without him signing it, then its terms are not the terms of a contract, but the conditions of his enslavement. If a government can be said to be moral because it is a Constitutional Republic, then a lynching may be said to be moral because it is democratic. It is a great sin that we tell all persons, "If you commit the crime of being born within certain imaginary borders, then you become the property of whichever imaginary entity and of whichever persons pretend to have authority over you."

*   *   *

It's fortunate that God constructed the world as He did. When we commit moral actions, they have an objectively good result on the world around us, and when we commit misdeeds, they have a deleterious effect. If not for this, it would be a sad reality indeed. We would have to make the difficult decision as to whether we should commit good deeds knowing that they will make the world worse off, or to commit misdeeds because we know that they will do good in the long run. This probably seems true to you, because you were taught the opposite. You were taught such lies as, "FDR did the right thing by murdering hundreds of thousands of innocent Japanese and German civilians, because it saved lives." You are conditioned to think that the world is a paradox wherein bad actions are actually good, but only if enacted under the beneficence of an all-knowing ruler (if private citizens were to do the same things for the same reasons, however, it would be bad). When properly fact-checking the histories of the world, it will inevitably be found that moral right coincides with factual right. Because "government" actions are necessarily violent and hence morally wrong, they are also factually wrong; that is to say, they do not bring about the good results that they are meant to, and in fact have a negative effect on the world. One such act is welfare, wherein "government" steals money from certain persons to give it to others. I

24

have no doubt that everyone involved in the distribution of welfare has only good intentions; otherwise the road to Hell would be unpaved.

As a struggling worker myself, I understand that life can be difficult and finances can be very tight. I once almost became homeless because I got downsized and was about to lose my apartment. Toward the end, I was selling my things and eating ramen to get by. Believe me when I say that my opposition to welfare has nothing to do with a lack of experience (an EBT card could have bought me some better food than 10-cent noodles) or a lack of sympathy. On the contrary, I oppose welfare out of sympathy. I realize that everyone would be much better off in the end without the violent distribution of money. I want the poor to cease being poor and I know that violence isn't the answer. I understand economics and history fairly well, which makes me the enemy of a great many persons. Learning how to recognize one's own bias and then trying to set it aside is very difficult even if you want to. But if you staunchly refuse to listen to reason because you're controlled by your emotions, there is very little, if any, hope for you. The following is a prime example of this.

(Note: This essay was originally written for a blog. Everything remains intact in print except for the hyperlinks of course. To follow these links, please visit the original blog post at cakescorner.me/2016/03/21/post101/3/)

On a blog of mine, I posted a graph showing the rise in welfare spending in the US. The content is pasted below. My blog's name in the following exchanges is "myhouseofrandom." When I posted this picture, I included the tagline, "Thanks, LBJ. Over $20 Trillion spent on the war on poverty so far, and poverty hasn't been reduced at all." The first stranger to have a dialogue with me is "entitledrichpeople."

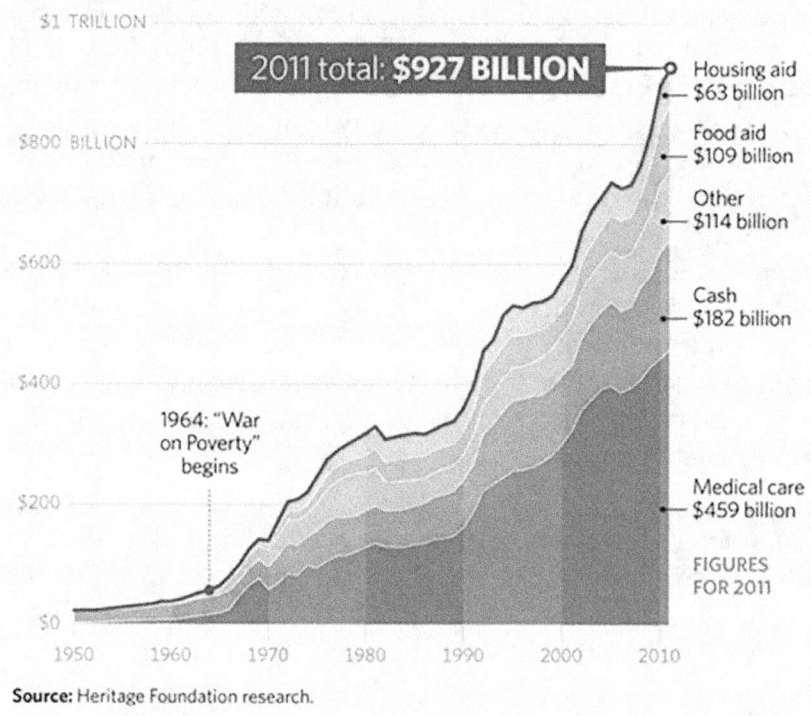

Welfare Spending Reaches Nearly $1 Trillion a Year

In 2011, the total cost of federal and state means-tested welfare programs was $927 billion, an all-time high. That includes over 80 federal programs but does not include spending on Social Security or Medicare. The amount is 16 times higher than it was in 1964 when the government began the "War on Poverty."

TOTAL WELFARE SPENDING, IN 2011 INFLATION-ADJUSTED DOLLARS

$1 TRILLION

2011 total: **$927 BILLION**

Housing aid
$63 billion

Food aid
$109 billion

Other
$114 billion

$800 BILLION

Cash
$182 billion

$600

$400

1964: "War
on Poverty"
begins

Medical care
$459 billion

$200

FIGURES
FOR 2011

$0

1950   1960   1970   1980   1990   2000   2010

Source: Heritage Foundation research.

☎ heritage.org

In response to this graph, entitledrichpeople wrote:

[image description: a bulls**t graph about "1 Trillion in Welfare Spending"]

The idea that poor people getting food, health care, running water, electricity, indoor plumbing, and housing *gasp* is meaningless if the poverty rate remains unchanged means this person is okay with poor people literally starving, dying form [sic] *lack of health care, having* *no shelter, etc. And even more than that, that poor people mean so little that alleviation of suffering means nothing, nothing at all.*

Here's the explanation of why this chart is not only misleading but rather total bull**** is available here (this link doesn't note how blatantly racist it is that the misleading numbers include virtually all BIA spending, but I'm noting it).
Here's a discussion of the readily observable fact that LBJ's programs were gutted starting with Nixon, and that they actually did lower poverty rates significantly when they all existed and had funding, but that even the gutted programs improved wellbeing on a number of measures. During the 6 years the LBJ programs were fully funded, poverty dropped 43%. In 6 years.

But even beyond that, I went to a school build [sic] by the Johnson administration, know people who lived without running water, electricity, or health care before the 60s. A while ago I had a coworker who yelled at everyone who badmouthed LBJ because before his administration she lived in a house without electricity and running water and helped her mother give birth at home. And the "War on Poverty" you find so laughable changed all of that for her.
Not to excuse his horrible violent racist foreign policy, but LBJ could win an election in Appalachia tomorrow.

Poor people's lives and wellbeing matter, not just as abstract measures of national economics, but as real human beings that have needs and feelings and value. So yes, thanks, LBJ, for the War on Poverty. It saves lives. (Not so much thanks for escalating the war in Vietnam that was horrible, genocidal, and a violation of human rights).

Ignoring the fact that there is no real difference between violence used in Vietnam versus violence used in the US, I wrote the following response:

myhouseofrandom:

27

I was quite taken aback by your response for several reasons, not least of which for its vehement attack on my character. Just as with most other progressives who've spoken to me over the years, you seem to be intolerant of views that challenge your own and fairly arrogant in your beliefs; and as a result fail to challenge your own beliefs–not fact-checking unless the source you use to fact-check tells you exactly what you want to hear. But aside from this, you assault the character of whomever disagrees with you. If I believe that welfare does not help the poor, then what do you think of me? You don't think that I'm well-intentioned but misled; you don't think that I'm loving but ignorant; no. You think that I want poor people to starve. This is alarming. I defy you, sir, to bring a single person of sound mind before me who truly wants the poverty-stricken to starve. The manner in which you attacked my character speaks volumes about your expectations and opinions of mankind. Progressivism truly is a religion of anger, hatred, and intolerance. I wouldn't be surprised if you considered your ideological opponents sub-human. I feel that you owe me an apology for so recklessly demeaning me. I was actually having a good day yesterday until I read your response to my post.

As for the rebuttal of these numbers, I invite you to re-read the article you linked to on InTheseTimes. In this article, the definition of welfare is given thus:

Merriam-Webster's dictionary defines "welfare" like this:

a: aid in the form of money or necessities for those in need

b: an agency or program through which such aid is distributed

In that same article, however, the author claims that other programs, such as education grants for poor students or cancer screenings in poor communities, don't count as welfare. If welfare is aid to the needy, as the dictionary says, then any program that is aimed at helping the needy can be considered welfare. (If we stick to this definition, incidentally, then it would be inconsistent to refer to corporate tax breaks as "corporate welfare" since they're not meant to help the poor). *The author also claims that some programs go to*

Americans who don't live below the poverty line; and some other programs such as upgrades to water lines benefit everyone whether poor, well-off, or rich; and therefore don't count as welfare. But if we look at the dictionary definition, welfare helps those in need. If people in a town are in need of new water lines and government monies fund them, then by this definition that would count as welfare. This means that either the definition of welfare that you endorsed is incorrect, or that the way you think about welfare is. Either way, the amounts of money depicted in the above graph accurately reflect the US government's welfare spending. Also, if you think that it's racist to include BIA spending as welfare, then you're saying that those people inherently aren't really in need–that would make you the racist, sir.

As to your second article attributing the war on poverty to a reduction in poverty, this is a fallacious argument. You assume that because a reduction in poverty happened during LBJ's administration, then it means that LBJ was responsible. If you look at the facts, however, you'll see that the poverty rate had been falling drastically since the end of the Great Depression and continued well into LBJ's administration.

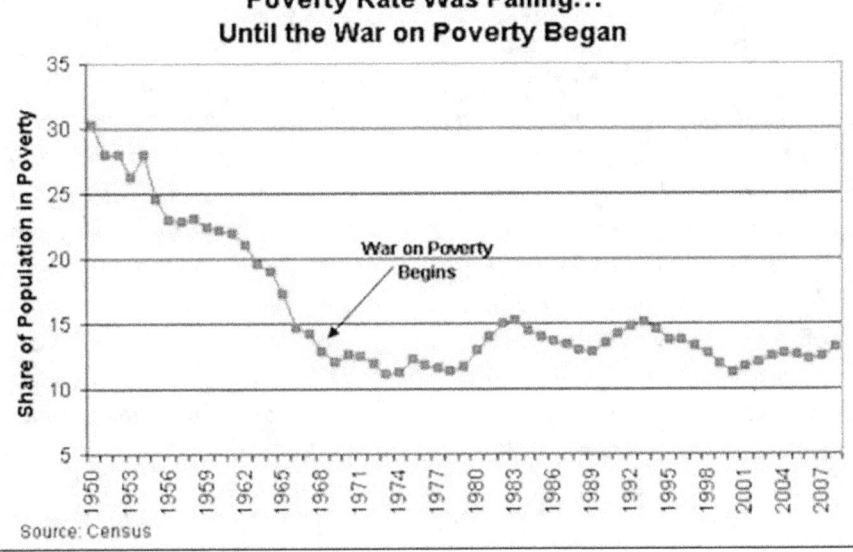

*If the level of poverty was in drastic decline before the war on poverty, then how can a further (temporary) reduction be credited to that very war? It's important to look at the big picture, not just a six-year timeframe. The big picture shows that poverty was reduced **before** the war on poverty but has not reduced in years **during** the war on poverty. How can you claim that the war on poverty was in any way a success when it has kept the poverty rate stagnant?*

*And your claim that Nixon "gutted" the welfare system is misleading at best. Nixon did reduce overall federal welfare spending and wished to get rid of it altogether, but only by replacing it with the Family Assistance Plan. Many Americans opposed the FAP because it would **increase** total welfare spending. |x| |x| If you want to focus on the destructive policies of Nixon, you ought to focus on policies that actually hurt the poor–the end of the gold standard, price and wage controls, runaway inflation–all policies of a big government interfering with the market. |x| |x|*

But even beyond that, I went to a school build by the Johnson administration, know people who lived without running water, electricity, or health care before the 60s.

Oh, wow. Anecdotal evidence–that's the best kind! The fact that you're bringing up Appalachia is laughable. Those states have always been poor precisely because of strong government interference. |x| |x| Mentioning that these states, especially WV, were poverty-stricken– when they were being crushed by government regulation–isn't helping your case at all. It only proves my point, that government interference in the market only hurts the poor. I believe that everyone should have access to electricity and running water. But I know that the market can provide services more cost-effectively and efficiently than government coercion, if only you'd let them.
Not only this, but it's insulting for you to say that it's ok to harm other people by taking money away from them, in order to give it to someone else a thousand miles away. Welfare doesn't work. |x| |x| |x| |x| |x| |x| |x| (And neither does any other government program. They only hurt the people they're trying to help.) But even if it did work, there would still be no moral justification for it. The ends do not justify the means. Stealing from one person to give to another is wrong, and nothing you

say, do, or think will ever make it stop being wrong. You are not entitled to another person's money. You sit there reading this on a computer that hundreds of millions of people across the globe could never afford, and yet you don't give away your money to them. If you have money in your bank account and spare change in your pocket then you are among the wealthiest 8% of people in the world. But I digress.

If anything I have written here has opened your eyes, I invite you to read more of what I've posted. A good place to start would be a research paper I wrote dealing with poverty |x| and another good resource for information would be the tag economics on my tumblog. If, on the other hand, your confirmation bias compels you to dismiss everything I have written because it doesn't fit in to your beliefs, then all I can say is good day, sir. I'll pray for you and ask God to change your heart. I hope that you'll learn to one day love your fellow man instead of hating them. It's not good for you.
Sincerely,

John

     I never heard a response from this fellow, but one of his followers was much more vocal. I submitted my above response to one of "entitledrichpeople's followers, "askawelfarecaseworker," because this person had reblogged his response and did not get a chance to read mine. I wanted to show both sides of the story, after all. This was the worker's response:

askawelfarecaseworker:

OK, first, not sure why you're submitting this instead of tagging me in it, or just letting the reblog sit, but….

entitledrichpeople is a poor person, with all the awfulness that generally entails. When you say to entitledrichpeople "welfare doesn't help poor people" or "we should eliminate welfare", you are actually saying "you don't know what helps you, and I want to take away the tools you use in order to feed yourself and get medical care."

That's what you're saying. Regardless of how well-intentioned you are, regardless of how "loving" you are – you are literally telling someone "I want to take away your groceries and your medical care, because you're not intelligent enough to know what's best for you".

And you get taken aback when that sentiment is met with anger?

I can't even understand why you thought your comment, or your response, would be met with anything else.

Something you should know about me is that I'm usually a very patient person. I am patient to a fault–it comes in handy when teaching small children how to play the violin and cello. My patience, however, is directly proportional to the purity of the motivations of the person I'm dealing with. If I sense that a person only wants to tell me off and uses straw man arguments or *ad hominem* attacks to do so, my sweet demeanor goes out the window pretty quickly. With that warning in place, here's what I wrote in response.
myhouseofrandom:

Wow, that is a complete and utter lie. I'm not saying that "I want to take away your groceries and medical care." I'm saying that I want to abolish welfare. You are assuming that if not for welfare, then people wouldn't be able to acquire anything, which is the complete opposite of the truth. It's a logical fallacy to say, "If not for X, then Y wouldn't happen at all" without considering the possibility of Z or some other letter providing Y. I demonstrated quite clearly that welfare is keeping people in poverty. If you cared about the truth then you would realize that, but you are appealing to your emotions instead.

Every dollar spent on welfare is a dollar not spent on creating jobs. The fact of the matter is that almost everyone who is poor, is poor because they are unemployed or underemployed. Those few who are employed full-time an [sic] still poor, are poor because of crushing taxes and regulations that make it extremely difficult to get ahead. If employers had a trillion dollars to employ people with, then those people would not only be getting money from their jobs, but they would also be producing something of value and adding to the economy. Is food expensive? Well if there were more workers being paid to produce food then food would be cheaper. If there were more people who could afford food because they have steady jobs, then there would be no lack of demand. It's really not a difficult concept to grasp as long as you're open-minded. But as I said, confirmation bias will compel you to dismiss everything I said.

And honestly, I wasn't expecting my comment or response to be met with anything else. As I said before, I've dealt with progressives before and their attitude is always the same. It's all gut reactions, logical fallacies, accusations, anger, hatred, and intolerance. That's what I've gotten from both of you over this post. I'm used to it by now.

What I've learned from worshipers of "government," who are so deeply entrenched in confirmation bias that they wouldn't admit their hair is on fire unless standing in front of a mirror, is that reading is difficult. It must be—no one I've ever debated has read what I've written or what I've linked to. That explains the next response.

You literally demonstrated nothing? [sic] There was no proof at all that welfare keeps people in poverty? [sic]

And since poor people such as entitledrichpeople get their groceries through food stamps and their medical care through Medicaid, you saying you want to abolish welfare – without actually suggesting any alternative in your original post, such as a universal basic income – IS saying "I want to take away your groceries and medical care".

You need to actually say what you think would be good, rather than just saying "the way you currently take care of yourself is bad".

Also, you're still being really paternalistic and patronizing and telling poor people they don't know what's best for themselves, so please stop that. entitledrichpeople knows better than you what poor people need, since they are actually poor and living their life with government aid. I know better than you what poor people need because I lived on government aid and I'm still trying to climb out of the mountain of debt I incurred just trying to pay my rent and treat my asthma.

Listen to us before you go off making up random, untested theories about what poor people need and how poor people don't understand how government aid hurts them.

And my rebuttal:

Oh my goodness. You really need to work on your reading comprehension skills, love. In my previous response I did in fact provide much evidence that welfare keeps people in poverty.
*The big picture shows that poverty was reduced **before** the war on poverty but has not reduced in years **during** the war on poverty. How can you claim that the war on poverty was in any way a success when it has kept the poverty rate stagnant?*

Welfare doesn't work. |x| |x| |x| |x| |x| |x| |x| (And neither does any other government program. They only hurt the people they're trying to help.)
Now, I'll give you the benefit of the doubt and say that you either forgot about that, or didn't realize that those x's were all links. But there is your evidence. If that's not enough, then here's some more evidence: |x| |x| |x| |x| |x| |x| |x| |x| |x| |x| |x| |x| |x| |x| |x| It's overwhelmingly clear that welfare hurts the very people it's trying to help.
But I can't give you the benefit of the doubt in your next claim—that I offered no alternative to welfare. Writing about the alternative made up about half of my most recent response.

Every dollar spent on welfare is a dollar not spent on creating jobs. The fact of the matter is that almost everyone who is poor, is poor because they are unemployed or underemployed. Those few who are employed full-time an still poor, are poor because of crushing taxes and regulations that make it extremely difficult to get ahead. If employers had a trillion dollars to employ people with, then those people would not only be getting money from their jobs, but they would also be producing something of value and adding to the economy. Is food expensive? Well if there were more workers being paid to produce food then food would be cheaper. If there were more people who could afford food because they have steady jobs, then there would be no lack of demand. It's really not a difficult concept to grasp as long as you're open-minded. But as I said, confirmation bias will compel you to dismiss everything I said.

Look at that. That paragraph is huge and you completely skipped over it. I clearly stated that full-time employment is the best alternative to welfare. (Another, of course, is charity |x| |x|.) Statistics from the BLS show that only 4% of all Americans who work full-time are in poverty. |x| Astoundingly, that number drops to 0.3% for full-time workers who have a high school diploma/GED and don't have children until they're married. To recap: If you work full-time, have a diploma, and wait to have children until after marriage, your chances of being poor are 0.3%. |x| The most effective way to eliminate poverty is to change your behavior, not to pick my pocket.

And that is the real issue behind the debate about government benefits. Government benefits stand in opposition to individual responsibility. It's really hard to get out of poverty (although it would be a whole lot easier without government interference) and I sympathize with anyone who is in poverty. What I do not sympathize with, however, is the belief that you have a right to someone else's money. I could have gone on welfare four years ago when I lost my job and my apartment, but I chose not to because I believe that slavery is wrong. Not only would I be a slave to government money, but I would also be enslaving others who work for a living and are having their paycheck plundered.

And why should I stop telling poor people what's best for them? You wouldn't have a problem with a doctor telling sick people what's best for them. Why the double standard? I'll tell you why: Because you fail to understand that economics is an actual science with laws and theorems. Sure economists are wrong sometimes just as doctors are wrong sometimes. But facts are facts no matter what people's opinions are. Economics is not a matter of "feeling." It doesn't matter how badly you feel for the poor. What matters is the truth; and the truth is that no amount of government spending can help the poor. In fact, that's the opposite of the truth. Whether you want to believe it or not doesn't change the facts. You can choose not to believe in gravity, but you'll still fall if you jump out a window.

Finally, let me point out that you're behaving exactly as I predicted you would.

It's all gut reactions, logical fallacies, accusations, anger, hatred, and intolerance.

You accuse me of not knowing what it's like to be poor, even though you know nothing about me. You're just making up assumptions and accusing me (while employing the logical fallacy "ad hominem," I might add). Of course, there's another characteristic of the progressive debater that I failed to mention: that is the inability to actually read what your opponent is writing and just ignore it, then reassert what you stated previously like a broken record. "You want people to starve!" *"Well, no, actually. I don't want people to starve. That's why I oppose this program."* "You want people to starve! You want people to starve! You want people to starve!" *Honestly, I would rather try to have an argument with a wind tunnel.*

Good day to you.

    I was really hoping that that was the end of it. I ought to have known better. Most people love to hear themselves talk (or watch themselves write, as it were). This person was far from finished. Here we go.

I'm cracking the hell up at this because, yes, I read you. You're not actually providing any viable alternatives, and you're just spouting random nonsense that doesn't add up to anything logical.

But oh, I'm supposedly the one talking about gut reactions and logical fallacies.

Let's start with this:

The War on Poverty has failed because conservative politicians gutted anti-poverty measures. AFDC was gutted in favor of TANF – with its 5 year LIFETIME limit and focus on job hunting (you have to do 20-30 hours a week of "job-related" activities to stay in compliance – which makes it harder for people to actually find a job, because they get sanctioned if they don't show up for their job program, even if they're missing it to do something like, oh, GO TO A JOB INTERVIEW.

Funding for actual skill-building, education, etc. has been slashed to the point where nothing productive can be provided. Again, this is not the fault of LBJ or any progressive politician that actually wants to fight poverty. This is the fault of conservative politicians gutting the programs.

Let's continue with this:

Every dollar spent on welfare is a dollar not spent on creating jobs. The fact of the matter is that almost everyone who is poor, is poor because they are unemployed or underemployed. Those few who are employed full-time an still poor, are poor because of crushing taxes and regulations that make it extremely difficult to get ahead. If employers had a trillion dollars to employ people with, then those people would not only be getting money from their jobs, but they would also be producing something of value and adding to the economy.

This is all nonsense. First of all, you're ignoring the existence of disabled people. Second, you're ignoring the fact that unemployment is a standard part of capitalism – that's how it works. This is literally in any economics textbook, so I'm not sure how you missed it.

Plus, this idea that removing taxes creates jobs because now employers have more money to throw around? You can't be serious. Especially when CEO pay is at an all-time high, while worker wages are stagnant and the minimum wage is falling in value. CORPORATIONS ALREADY HAVE MONEY. It's just going to the CEO instead of job creation or worker pay.
Not to mention only 11% of tax revenue goes toward safety net programs, so eliminating welfare isn't actually going to lower your taxes that much. Getting rid of ALL taxes means getting rid of interstate highways, firefighters, police officers, public parks, etc. IDK about you, but I like being able to easily drive out of state to visit my family. I like hiking and enjoying public works for free. I like that I got

to go to a state-run school instead of having to try to pay $20k a semester for private tuition. None of that would be possible without taxes.

And the idea that a minimum-wage worker wouldn't be in poverty if taxes were eliminated? Federal minimum wage is $7.25/hr. That's $1160/mo. Have you tried to survive on that? That's about the net amount I took home from my first post-college full-time job, and let me tell you, it wasn't sustainable. Between rent, groceries, phone bill, and electricity, I was out of money within a week of being paid – and that's even before my student loan payment. I can't even imagine how impossible it would have been if I had had kids.

Also you've fundamentally misunderstood slavery if you think welfare is in any way comparable. Let me give you a hint: The worst thing that can happen to you while on welfare is losing your welfare. Your caseworker doesn't own you. You're free to walk away at any point. If you get a job that pays well enough, you walk away without being forced to do anything else. Slavery? Is actually nothing like that. There's descriptions of the reality of slavery in most history textbooks, and firsthand accounts of actual slaves out there if you really want an accurate picture (and none of them contain the phrase "It was just like receiving cash assistance from the government!").

I read your points earlier. I just summarily dismissed them as the nonsense unreality that they were.

You're still being patronizing and lecturing poor people on what's best for them – which needs to stop. You're still assuming you know better than poor people – when you have no idea how taxes, welfare, or the free market works.

Just. Stop. Read some actual sources, do some actual critical thinking, and please don't respond again unless you actually get some context and stop living in Ayn Rand's fantasy world.

I remember it took me over an hour to write the following response because of all the sources I had to dig up from the bowels of my archives. That was not fun at all. I had things to do that morning. So, I ignored the fact that this person is ableist because they think that disabled people can't find work, but I was going for the big points. Here's that.

Congratulations, you've written the stupidest thing I've ever read.

If you were interested in the truth and you wanted to listen to me explain these things to you, I would be happy to do so. But because you think that you already know everything, you can't be convinced of anything. And considering how quickly you wrote this response, it's obvious that you didn't devote any serious time to reading and digesting my previous posts or my cited sources.

First off, entitlement spending has not been gutted. As the graph in my original post shows, entitlement spending has only been increasing. In the late 1960's it was 6% of GDP and is now 15%. |x| And a job interview doesn't take 140 hours. If you only have to work 30 hours a week for this program and you have a job interview, that's not going to be impossible in your schedule. Nice try.
Capitalism causes TEMPORARY unemployment. It doesn't destroy jobs, it only relocates them |x|. Millions of Americans became unemployed when the automobile became popular, but it didn't last. You see, before the automobile up to a third of all American crops were grown just to feed horses. Millions of Americans were employed just for horses–to breed them, to raise them, to train them, to feed them, to clean them, to fit them with horse shoes, etc. Yet you didn't hear about long unemployment lines in the early 20th century. This is because those Americans previously employed for horses went on to be employed elsewhere. They went on to build gas stations, to erect stoplights, to build cars, to wash cars or fix cars, to become taxi drivers or driving instructors. Capitalism shifted employment because cars are more useful to us than horses. It is true that the ultimate goal of capitalism is to create permanent unemployment for everyone, because employment only exists to satisfy our need for scarce resources. I am quite familiar with economics, thank you.

Predictably, you fall on tired old economic myths and misunderstandings to support your feeble beliefs. If you were to read anything in my tag economics on my blog you would see that I've already written or posted rebuttals to everything you've written. But as I said before, you're not open-minded and you have no interest in challenging your own beliefs. It doesn't matter that CEOs are making a lot of money because it doesn't come at the expense of everyone else. |x| Saying that workers' wages are stagnant is greatly misleading. |x| And most companies don't have nearly as much money as you think. |x| Sure, there are multi-billion dollar corporations, but there are also multi-billionaire people. The average CEO makes slightly more money than the average dentist. |x| Also, the evidence is insurmountable that minimum wage kills jobs. |x| |x| |x| |x| |x| |x| |x| |x| |x| |x| |x| |x| |x| |x| |x| |x| |x| |x| |x| |x| |x| |x| |x| |x| |x| You would know this already if you had read through the posts on my blog like I asked.

And now comes the next logical fallacy: If not for government, there wouldn't be X. Two posts ago I pointed out that this was a fallacy and said that there were alternatives. Last post I repeated this and was much clearer about why this is fallacious. And here you are repeating it again, just as I said you would:

that is the inability to actually read what your opponent is writing and just ignore it, then reassert what you stated previously like a broken record.

So here you are again with that fallacy, assuming that without the government, then X wouldn't get done. This is absurd. Before the 20th century virtually all roads in the US were privately built and owned. Today in Sweden, two-thirds of all roads are privately built and owned–and the private roads are in much better condition, for less maintenance cost than public roads, and with much less traffic volume. |x| Not only can we do things without the government, we can do them a whole lot better than the government!

Your claim that only 11% of spending goes to welfare is dubious |x| but aside from that it's a red herring. I said that if we had $1 Trillion less spending, then we would have an extra $1 Trillion. That's not really something that can be disputed; it's simple math. If we had an extra $1 Trillion to spend on creating jobs for 8.3 Million |x| unemployed Americans, we could pay them each $120,000 per year, *assuming no overhead. If they were working, then they would be producing something of value and adding value to the economy. Economic growth is the primary mechanism whereby the poor are lifted out of poverty |x| |x| |x| |x| If more people work and make the economy bigger, everyone else will benefit.*

Also, minimum wage pays more than poverty. The poverty line is currently defined as being around $11K and minimum wage pays about $15K. To earn less than poverty wages you would have to work minimum wage for less than 32 hours a week. |x| And to answer your question, yes I have tried to live off of $1,000 per month. It was difficult. I had to ride the bus everywhere and I couldn't ever eat out because it was too expensive. I had to make a lot of concessions, give up most of my luxuries, and even do without a few important things like new glasses. But I survived. As I said before, I do have sympathy for everyone who is poor. But I don't have sympathy for an attitude of entitlement.

As to your description of slavery, I must point out that your definition is terribly limited. I'm not going to try to explain it to you because I know that you won't read it anyway. I know this for a fact because I said before that you only ignore me and repeat yourself like a broken record. You proved me correct when you wrote:

You're still being patronizing and lecturing poor people on what's best for them – which needs to stop.

Now, I responded to this last time and wondered why this is a problem. You didn't say why it's a bad thing, you just told me that I need to stop. And then you told me again, like a broken record.

Like a broken record.

Like a broken record.

[END]

My favorite moment from the argument was writing this: "*the evidence is insurmountable that minimum wage kills jobs. |x| |x| |x| |x|*

$|x|$ $|x|$ $|x|$ $|x|$ $|x|$ $|x|$ $|x|$ $|x|$ $|x|$ $|x|$ $|x|$ $|x|$ $|x|$ $|x|$ $|x|$ $|x|$ $|x|$ $|x|$ $|x|$ $|x|$ $|x|$" That was really satisfying. Look at all those beautiful x's. Anyway, I'm certain that this person did respond to my post again, although I don't know what they wrote because I refused to read it. I won't let someone waste any more of my time if they insist on being that stupid. Just to be clear, stupidity has nothing to do with how much you know; it has to do with how little you choose to know. Anyone can be forgiven for being ignorant of economics. There's a lot that I don't know. There are even things that Frederic Bastiat or Ludwig von Mises didn't know. But the unwillingness to learn and admit that you're wrong will make you stupid. And that is the case here.

Please learn from this and don't repeat the same mistakes. If there's a cause you're passionate about, challenge yourself before you challenge others. Ask, "Is my cause really a good one? How do I know? Am I trying to accomplish it by good means or evil means? Am I an imbecile?" After this, continue to attempt to discredit your beliefs. You'll definitely miss an argument the first few times and think your beliefs are good, but if you keep at it you'll discover some falsity you missed before. Everyone is very good at criticizing other persons' beliefs, but very few are good at criticizing their own. This is because we believe that if we feel something, then it's true. So stop it. You'll be doing yourself and others a great service by realizing that facts are independent of your feelings.

If your eyes have been opened and you want to learn more, there are many good resources below for you to check out. Some are easy to digest and some are rather nebulous, so be forewarned.

(Note: These recommended media are hyperlinked on my blog cakescorner.me/2016/03/21/post101/3/ but they can also be searched for online.)

The State

Punching Holes in the Public Goods Argument by Tracey Zoeller (article, 2,700 words)
Four Things the State Is Not by Thomas Woods, Jr. (video, 59:43)
Anatomy of the State by Murray Rothbard (book, 62 pages)
The Law by Frederic Bastiat (book, 107 pages)

Statism

Statism: The Most Dangerous Religion by Larken Rose (video, 12:35)
"It Can't Happen Here!" by Larken Rose (video, 1:34:23)
No Treason by Lysander Spooner (book, 51 pages)

Economics & History

Economics in One Lesson by Henry Hazlitt (book, 198 pages)
Myths that Conceal Reality by Milton Friedman (video, 52:43)
Applying Economics to American History by Tom Woods, Jr. (video, 36:48)
Free to Choose by Milton Friedman (video- 10 part series, ~10 hours)
The Politically Incorrect Guide to US History by Tom Woods, Jr. (book, 270 pages)
America's Great Depression by Murray Rothbard (book, 411 pages)

Additional Resources

Please excuse the self-promotion, but it's easy for me to consolidate things on my blog, and it saves me the trouble of having to update this list every time I find something new. When I post/reblog something new on blogspot, the following links will include them so there's no need to come searching here.

http://myhouseofrandom.blogspot.com/search/label/economics
http://myhouseofrandom.blogspot.com/search/label/government
http://myhouseofrandom.blogspot.com/search/label/politics
http://myhouseofrandom.blogspot.com/search/label/history

A Rebuttal to Myself

by John "**This** time I'm correct" Everett
2014/02/26

(Note: This is a rebuttal to a paper I had written three years prior. In the original paper, I argued that the government has a responsibility to ban same-sex marriage in order to protect religious rights. I like to use this paper and its rebuttal as a perfect example of how my beliefs have changed over time. I no longer support the idea of government because I have grown, learned, and then repented of my false beliefs. I expect the same of everyone else.)

There is a very strong tendency for humans to submit to an "us vs. them" mentality. It is believed that this mentality long kept us safe from foreign invaders and pathogens. In the absence of antibiotics it would be all too easy for a member from a different tribe or clan to infect a whole village. Thus the tendency to separate ourselves has continued through all of history, even going so far as to create rivalries between different ideologies. What makes it nonsensical is that we often form rifts between two ideologies that are nearly the same. The "us vs. them" mentality causes us to exaggerate differences and exaggerate negatives. Consider this: If you drive to work one morning and a car cuts you off on the freeway, that event will likely stick out in your mind. The problem with this is forgetting about the 5,000 other cars that *didn't* cut you off, and forgetting about the 5,000 drivers who perhaps are neither very safe nor particularly dangerous drivers–they **have** to be either good or bad, darn it! We can't accept middle ground, and that could be why the movie "Waterworld" is infamous. It was disappointing but it wasn't a terrible movie, and that frustrates us. We instinctively get a kick out of conflict, perhaps because it makes us feel like good guys, and we want to feel as though we're fighting a just and fair crusade against the forces of darkness. Light and dark; no middle. So what we end up doing is separating someone whose beliefs may be quite similar to ours, refusing to believe that there could be a third option, hyperbolizing the "light" and "dark," and focusing on their difference. We then end up locked in a struggle between 99 and 100. Those two numbers are different by a whole **1%**! How could you not pick a side!? Which brings me to the Republican and Democratic parties.

DEMOCRATS | REPUBLICANS

WILL LIE TO YOU AND STEAL YOUR MONEY   **WILL LIE TO YOU AND STEAL YOUR MONEY**

In our two party system, the two reigning parties are seen as polar opposites, being referred to as the "left" and "right." Any compromise between the two is considered the "middle ground." You can't get much more different than that! Of course, this assumes that there is no other option. When you look at the essence of (modern-day) Republican and Democratic views, you'll see that they are the same–the only difference lies in how the parties want to manage their rule. Last year Republicans wanted to raise food stamp spending by 57% while Democrats wanted to raise it by 65%. That might seem like a huge disparity but when you compare the end results, $725 Billion instead of $764 Billion, you'll see that the difference is only $39 Billion, or 5.2%. Keep that in mind for this next part. When you get married you sign a marriage license and the state "allows" you to be married. When you file your taxes there are different rules for single persons and married couples. The government *regulates* marriage, here meaning "prescribes the legal limits within which it is allowed." There is a fine line separating a ban from regulation, because regulatory limits define how marriage is viewed by the state (i.e. if you don't sign a marriage license, the state considers you unmarried, but they won't arrest you for it). Here the separation between the "left" and "right" views seems quite large. But when you think about what they have in common you'll see mostly agreement. Refer to the handy chart below for clarification.

	★★★ (elephant)	(donkey)
Government control and regulation of marriage	☑	☑
Same-sex marriage	☒	☑
Polygamous marriage	☒	☒
Incestuous marriage	☒	☒
Pedophilic marriage	☒	☒
Marriage to a large soda	☒	☒
		(In New York, small sodas are allowed.)

(If you don't get the joke: Democratic mayor of New York, Michael Bloomberg, banned large sodas in 2012—the ban was overturned by New York state's highest court in 2014.)

The "middle ground" wants the decision to be left up to state governments. But don't forget that it's possible to have a fourth option! The fourth option is this: no government ought to regulate marriage because it is a religious institution and ought to be reserved to the people themselves. Unfortunately we have been conditioned to think inside the box. When someone asks you "Do you support gay marriage," what they are really asking is "How do you want the government to control religious institutions?" That question assumes that government ought to control religion, and the only difference is an opinion as to *how* the government ought to control our lives. This is merely an illusion of choice. In the end, no matter whether you choose the Republican or Democratic belief, nothing will change for the government; they will still be in control of your religion. In my opinion this false dichotomy exists only for the purpose of keeping us divided and seeing each other as the enemy. "To divide and conquer" is the oldest trick in the book. In feudal Europe and Japan the people would fight each other over land in a never-ending game of tug-of-war. When they saw each other as the enemy, the ruler didn't need to fear an uprising. Such conflicts would only distract the people so that the government could continue to rule over them. This is the same situation we face today. If we do not realize that the only conflict is between liberty and tyranny, the people and the ruling class, then we won't upset the established order that has been decided for us.

My mistake in claiming that the government ought to regulate marriage for the sake of protecting religious rights was hinged upon a fundamental misunderstanding of the government's proper role in society. The first amendment, when stating that "Congress shall make no law respecting the establishment of a religion, or prohibiting the free exercise thereof," specifically prohibits the government from ruling over religious matters. The government's role is not to protect so-called "religious rights" from private offenders, but rather to prevent the government itself from violating religious rights. "The constitution is not an instrument for the government to restrain the people, it is an instrument for the people to restrain the government- lest it come to dominate our lives and interests." -Patrick Henry

When the government made gay marriage illegal, it broke the law by prohibiting the free exercise of religion. Marriage is a matter of the church to decide, not the state. Suppose the state were to make eating pork illegal, because Jews, Muslims, and Hindus believe that such consumption is wrong. It would be absurd to suggest that the government would have any right to regulate what we put in our bodies just because many people consider it wrong. The government's only proper role is to restrain us from causing physical harm to others, and otherwise leaving us free to manage our own affairs. It is not proper for the government to limit an activity simply because it is wrong. Being gay is wrong? Well so is lying, so should you be in jail right now? We would have near-universal imprisonment for our sins. Is there anyone who has never been proud, coveted another person's possessions, or erupted in anger without due cause? These are all sins, yet it would be foolish for the government to try to enforce such laws. The law of man is not the Law of God, nor should it be. Jesus never said that the Roman government should crack down on offenses against God. He didn't ever try to have anyone arrested (my goodness, when His own disciple *cut off a man's ear* He didn't shriek in anger). Why do Christians who profess to love God not do his work? Why must we depend on the state to do the church's work (or what we imagine to be the church's work)? Banning gay marriage isn't going to stop homosexuality from existing; all it can do is appease our twisted conscience. The problem is not that the state is "letting" someone have freedom– in fact, I'm pretty sure the desire to be free is why we seceded from Britain back in 1776. The problem is within the hearts of men and no law will ever change the heart of man. Society's problem is not the state's problem.

Perhaps the so-called "decay of morality" comes largely from the belief that charity ought to come from the state. Rather than witnessing to others we ought to just have the state ban everything that we don't like. Rather than donating money ourselves we ought to just have the state steal from people so it can write welfare checks–and fifty years after the War on Poverty started, the poor are still poor! Imagine that! Forcing morality on others doesn't give anyone any incentive to improve! When you look at the facts there is no valid reason to ban gay marriage, or drugs, or paying employees below $7.25 per hour, or anything else that doesn't cause physical harm to another. Charity begins at home. Perhaps you ought to have your own house in order before you try to tidy someone else's. True, being gay is a sin. So what? Forcing your fellow man to live his life the way you want instead of the way he wants is also a sin. I believe the word for that is "slavery." So cry me a river, build a bridge, and get over it.

There is, of course, one more very important point to consider when it comes to legal sanction/prohibition. When the government is in charge of marriage instead of private parties, the government gets to dictate how we are required to behave in regards to marriage. If the state had no involvement in marriage, believers would be perfectly free under the law to refuse recognition of any marriage they deemed sinful or invalid. But when the state is involved, anti-discriminatory laws will force believers to either act against their religious beliefs or receive

48

punishment. Last year a baker in Oregon (in)famously refused to bake a wedding cake for a gay couple and faced an investigation. The baker, Klein, said of the matter, "I believe that marriage is a religious institution ordained by God. A man should leave his mother and father and cling to his wife … that to me is the beginning of marriage." When asked if he would be willing to lose his business license, he said, "If I have to be to, I guess, be penalized for my beliefs, then I guess, well, that'll be what it is." No man should ever have to choose between his beliefs and the law. I say this not only from a moral standpoint but also a logical one.

Let's assume that homosexuality is instead perfectly fine and this baker is in the wrong; let's assume also that the state has no involvement in the matter. What do you suppose could happen? This baker would lose business from all potential gay patrons, who might organize a boycott. If the community is passionate enough about the issue you would see many, many straight customers deny him business and he would lose a lot of money for his stance—all without legislation. When the government makes anti-discriminatory laws they are forcing "prejudiced" businessmen to hide their beliefs. This happened today in Arizona, as a matter of fact. Now instead of customers being aware of the businessman's beliefs and choosing to avoid patronizing it, they are now being forced, in a manner of speaking, to give their money to that businessman because they are unaware of his beliefs. Whom do anti-discriminatory laws protect besides discriminators, and what falls under the category of discrimination, anyway?

Oh, and by the way, the word "bigotry" means "the refusal to respect beliefs that differ from one's own." When you call someone a bigot for not having the same beliefs as you, it's actually the case that **you** are the bigot, not them. Please use words correctly.

Going even further back in time, the next writing (more of a rant, really) gives you a glimpse into my still-changing and inconsistent mind. I first learned about the idea of limited government in October of 2012 at the height of the election season. In January of 2013 when this was written, I was still slowly making my journey into libertarianism. Now, of course, I am fully anti-government and have been since 2014 or 2015. Being able to read this below writing is like looking into a time capsule. It's a curious glimpse into the uncomfortably inconsistent and dissonant thinking that resulted from my mind becoming an ideological battleground. You may find it interesting as well. Just don't believe any of it—not even the title.

Free Coffee Coupons!
Inquire Within!

OK, That title was the bait, now time for the switch.

I decided to try something a little different with the way I discuss things and wrote this monologue as I thought it up. As with any free writing exercise, I started typing and didn't stop until I was done; essentially producing a stream of consciousness diatribe. It's guaranteed more invigorating than a nice cup of tea (once you're down to just the leaves)! Anyway, I didn't change any words since finishing. I only added punctuation, edited spelling, etc.

The government is a paradox. It's meant to rule over worldly mundane matters and so a government by its very definition is secular, yet it is through this tool that we are able to do God's work. Consider what Hobbes said about life, that without government life would be nasty, brutish, and short. The government is the result of a community banding together to rule over earthly matters together for the benefit of all. Because the presence of a government coordinates things, brings about order, and stuff like that our lifespans increase. There is more safety, in theory, and we can better reach out to those around us to do God's work. When a well-maintained government is in place, our lifespans increase and when we are older, we are wiser. When we're wiser, we can better advise those younger than us on how to live a proper life. When we are old we have both experience and authority, and the older we are the more experience we have. By creating a government to rule over worldly matters, we are assisting spiritual matters. When you have the stability that comes from a governed society you have innovation. The Romans had the aqueducts and the Arabians had glass work. Throughout human history the needle is always moving up. First there were the roads, and then there was travel by horses, and then there was steam communication, and then there was the telegram, and then there was the telephone, and then the computer and then the internet, and then the World Wide Web. All these thousands of years have led us slowly, yet surely, forward toward all the benefits that we have now. Thanks to the existence of the Web, we can now disseminate information globally. Anyone who can read and has access to a computer with a dial-up connection can read the Bible. There are more Christians alive today than there have been throughout the last two thousand years combined.

This would not have been possible without us dwelling on earthly affairs and keeping ourselves safe from those who would harm us, and, as Hammurabi said, to create a rule of righteousness in the land, so that the strong should not harm the weak. But in order to do this, we have to have that enforcement, provided by our militia, and the military. Herein lies another contradiction, for in keeping a well-regulated militia we must take up arms against our neighbors when they threaten our safety. Jesus said "Do not resist an evil man. If any man striketh thee upon the right cheek, turn to him the other." To support the military is to support those who fight in order to protect our freedoms out of their own goodwill and selflessness, yet it also means that we are to support those who would take another person's life without a second thought. And are we to protect our families by subduing those who threaten their life and limb, yet in the same breath proclaim that life is an inalienable right? It is a paradox that we should consider it necessary to protect ourselves with firearms, yet preach against violence. Yet if it were not for the willingness to take up arms against threats, then we would not be allowed the freedom to do so if we chose. If the Libyan people had not drawn their guns, they would still be under the oppressive rule of Qaddafi. Thus—at least it seems so—we must sacrifice a part of our spiritual purity in order to ensure the continued enjoyment of the freedoms that God gave to all men and that governments are charged with preserving.

So peace is also a paradox, for the threat or execution of violence is what preserves peace. The philosopher Aristotle said "We make war so that we can have peace." Vegetius said "Si vis pacem, para bellum." Thousands of years later George Washington echoed these sentiments by saying "Being prepared for war is the most effective way to ensure peace." The peace of God surpasses all, but the peace of Earth is fragile and subject to the most transient of temperaments. In order to maintain the peace of Earth, we must maintain the elements of war. To keep something earthly, we must exercise something else earthly. It's like, if you tell a lie, you have to tell more lies to maintain it. If you want something earthly, you have to keep being earthly to maintain it.

But if it were not for looking toward earthly things, we would not have the luxury of taking care of spiritual things. Buddha said "To keep the body healthy is a duty, otherwise we cannot keep our minds strong and clear." If not for sweating inside a stuffy building during the summer, the US's founding fathers would not have written the constitution that properly limits the government's power, keeping us safe from tyranny. In a manner of speaking, the government is like the body, which must be taken care of with the fruits of the earth before the spirit can have time to flourish. If the government continues to exist the needle will continue to move up. We will continue to live longer, God's word will continue to spread and be taught (provided we don't let such a freedom be denied us), and the general quality of life, that thing most conducive to comfortable invention, will rise.

But why should the standard of living go up? We are too rich. We have every physical need taken care of and we want for nothing. We are lazy, practically useless, and entitled. If you do not have a car today, you are considered below the curve. If you do not have a washer and dryer you are poor. If you do not have a refrigerator, your dietary options are severely limited. But there's the thing. If not for the invention of the refrigerator, many people would have died of food poisoning in the last century. If not for modern technology, non-perishables such as canned foods and packaged dry foods would not be an option. If not for non-perishables, truly poor persons would surely starve to death. And this brings us full-circle. If not for the success of a worldly, concerned-with-

53

matters-of-the-physical society, we would not be able to feed the hungry. And it is impossible to think that God or nature should want for the hungry to be unfed just because the idea of government is inherently ungodly. The farmer who has his hands down in the muck and mud provides food for others, and in providing a necessary service he does good in God's eyes. And the capitalist, by ensuring that everyone is able to afford their necessary food, does just as much good.

But as I was saying firstly in the last paragraph, the innovations of society force us to be rich. In some cities you can live without a car, sure. But in most places you can't. And heaven forbid that you choose to not have a house. There's a guy who lives in a cave and he seems happy, but that is almost unheard of in this day and age. Why is it that, in order to function, you have to have luxuries? Basically what I'm trying to say is that it's hard to be focused on spiritual matters and improve yourself on the inside when an entire commercial society is shouting at you to improve your outside. The government, being made up of the people, responds in turn by setting minimum standards of poverty and digitizing everything. It can be sickening, tiring, to live day in and day out in a society that was built on the back of greed, while simultaneously feeling defeated because you realize that if not for such greed, you would probably be coughing up your lungs and dying in a gutter somewhere. And then what use could you be to anyone? How could you do God's work—or indeed, anyone's work, when you are a victim of a poor, wretched civilization?

We have the printing press because of a safe society that was protected by knights from bands of roving robbers. But does that mean we should all be a part of that society? Surely there must be some way that any one of us can reject the worldly matters and leave them to someone else. After all, if only one per cent of us choose to be vagrants like Jesus was, traveling and preaching the word and doing good while caring not for matters of the worldly or of the government, could not the other 99 per cent handle that stress? I'm just wondering that to myself. I don't think it would work because it's unheard of, just like that fellow in the cave, and society wouldn't know how to deal with it. I mean, if you have a disability there's paperwork and accommodations to be made and it's all ready because having a disability is not unheard of and society has a whole infrastructure set up to accommodate you. But to live outside of normal society and to care not for worldly matters? That is unheard of. How would society welcome you? How would they be able to communicate with you if you don't have a smart phone? Our entire modern society is built on memes of cats. You can't just ignore that and expect to get away with it.

So what to do?

-Join a convent and forget about the world outside. It doesn't matter anyway.

-Kill yourself.

-Kill everyone else. Just leave your car running until we all die of CO poisoning.

-Escape into a fantasy world inside your head.

-Make a fictional society where the government is not a paradox. Somehow.

-Go to the bottom of the ocean and build a new world called Rapture.

-Go to Mars and start your own colony where all of your loyal subjects are cats.

Actually, that last one was perfect. Become the King of Martian Cats.

Me gusta.

This rant, by the way, is a taste of what goes on in my brain, all day, every day. When I was waiting in line at McDonald's once, my mom saw that I looked pensive and asked me what I was thinking about. While still staring off into space, I calmly answered "The effects of nanotechnology on child-rearing." She wasn't quite sure what to make of that. I can assure you that you do not want to be me. The voices! The philosophical, inquisitive voices! Make them stop! Always thinking and pondering and wondering and pie! Mmm, pie. Pie pie pie. Piiiieeee. Peanut butter bacon chocolate. Oh, yes! Gasp! Eureka! Chocolate peanut butter cheesecake! Surely a food so wonderful could not exist within the realm of man, could it? The very universe should be torn asunder by its awesomeness. This I must meditate upon.

-Written January 17th, 2013

Update, January 31st— After some additional thought, I have concluded that a good, although not perfect compromise is to have a government that only dwells on earthly matters as much as it should. Socrates once said that philosophers are closer to death than anyone else, because they focus on their minds and spirits, only taking care of their bodies because it is necessary; meanwhile, brutes focus on their bodies, filling themselves with wine and song and all other things at their whim, and shun spiritual pursuits such as the search for truth. A republic such as the US has a government modeled around the idea of freedom, which is a spiritual concern. Notice how almost everything having to do with the so-called "American Way" is intangible. Life, liberty, and the pursuit of happiness are all ideas. A socialist government such as the USSR, on the other hand, is centered entirely on material. Everyone has the same wealth. Everyone has the same property (that is to say, none). Everyone is allotted a loaf of bread and state-issued boots. Everyone receives the same free, low quality healthcare. It's quite ironic that for all the Soviet talk of a greedy, capitalist America it is actually a socialist society that is terribly materialistic. I think it's very telling that in focusing on intangible matters, a capitalistic society ends up having both liberty *and* bread. True equality comes from equal protection under the law and equal opportunity to succeed. Whether we choose to be greedy or not is up to us.

Young persons tend to be more liberal because they are idealistic and think that providing equal measure of wealth will lead to prosperity (which is impossible) instead of poverty (which is invariably the result). As Cornel West said, "Too many young folk have addiction to superficial things and not enough conviction for substantial things like justice, truth, and love." Plato warned against the young being involved in politics because they were idealistic and more vulnerable to the charms of charismatic dictators such as Barack Obama. That's right. I went there. Please hold all impotent rage until the end of the ride. Moving on...

When decrying our bloated standard of living, it was rather naïve of me to suggest that the only two possibilities in life are a lavish, spoiled people; or starvation. We can all make the decision to have as much or as little as we can afford (or not afford). Actually, the more stuff we have, the less happy we are and the happier we are the longer we live, and right there is an example of how focusing less on the earthly will benefit you physically (in contrast to before where I said that focusing all on the earthly will help you out). That misapprehension can be attributed to my current immaturity. I'm only 22 years old–I still have much to learn. In essence, the less we choose to have, the better. The more we choose to give others (e.g. innovations, new technologies, apple pie) the better. In the end, the best situation is where we choose to live a dignified life of simple poverty, but are rich because of what others give us. I suppose a perfect world would be simultaneously capitalist and communist, but a perfect world would have no such terms for economics systems, nor would it have any government to regulate it. In reality, I can't honestly say what is the best way to go. Maybe join a sect of monks in the Alps. I hear they're beautiful this time of year. Actually, I'm really starting to like that King of Martian Cats idea.

A Vindication of the Rights of Babies

2011 April

Some debates go on for far too long.

With something complex like an economic issue or picking out sexy summer-wear, the length of argument can be frustrating, but when the debate is something that can be solved in minutes with the ever-elusive "logic" and "scientific reasoning," an argument's refusal to be resolved can be downright irritating. At this point in the paragraph, you're probably thinking "Just get to the point already!" Well, if you insist. The issue of which I speak is the long-going topic of abortion. I know, you want the argument to end too, right? I bet you don't even want to read this article anymore. But fear not, for I assure you I'll make it well worth your while. Throughout the article, I will refer to supporters of abortion as simply "proponents" for brevity's sake. So what do the proponents say to support abortion? The most common point they make is that an embryo is not alive. Rather than wax philosophic about that indescribable quality that makes us alive (or does it?), let's look at the characteristics found in every living organism to test this opinion.

Living organisms undergo a period of growth, maintain homeostasis, have a metabolism, respond to stimuli, reproduce, and, as a species, adapt to their environment. Since not every individual organism can reproduce (such as children and the infertile), only five of the above six characteristics are required to be met. Try as you may, you will never be able to find an embryo which does not meet all of the above criteria save reproduction. They grow (exponentially), they have organized bodies made up of cells, organs, and systems; they metabolize the nutrients sent by the mother via the umbilical cord (and transfer waste back to her the same way), respond to stimuli (how else would the zygote find the uterine wall to burrow in?), and, since they belong to the human species, share the same adaptation as all other humans simply by belonging to the species. Scientifically speaking, an embryo is alive. There is no religious debate, nor a philosophical one. Embryos are alive, and in the 21st century, believing that an embryo is not alive ought to be met with the same ridicule as thinking the Earth is flat.

And thus, many proponents do not dismiss an embryo's life, but merely its personhood. After all, an embryo cannot carry on a conversation, or sustain life independently of its mother (with current medical technology), or play *Mario Kart*, or do any of the things that persons can. Why, then, should they be called persons? Wouldn't a more accurate term be "growth" or even "parasite?" Embryos, by any measurable means, do not possess sentience, or even consciousness. They don't tap their tiny feet to the beat of music until well into the second trimester. Surely one could not refer to such a thing as a person! But if an embryo (meaning first-trimester baby) is not a person, then we must ask two questions. What, and When?

What is an embryo, if not a person? Is it a chipmunk, or is it human but not "person?" You may think the chipmunk question was in jest, but I assure you it is necessary to pose it with seriousness, in order to discuss all possible permutations of this argument, so let's get to the answer. Without over-thinking, what separates a human-type organism from an organism of the chipmunk class? If you answered "capacity for love" or "cheek size" I'm glad you succeeded in not over-thinking, but you missed the mark. What I was going for was "Human DNA." Humans are made of human organs, made of human cells containing strands of human DNA. Chipmunks, likewise, contain fuzzy rodent DNA. Whether a human is alive or not, he is still considered human. Thus when we see a human corpse, we don't say "Look at the size of that chipmunk!" but rather "How embarrassing; when I die, I hope I'm not wearing a Hannah Montana shirt like that guy." As silly as it is for me to distinguish a human from a chipmunk, it's important to establish that a human's embryo is human, if not a person, and thus is entitled to the same basic rights as any other human. Even after death, humans are protected by laws such as those prohibiting grave exhumation and necrophilia. So now that we've established that a human embryo is indeed human, does that alone make it a person? An embryo is human

59

and contains human cells with human DNA, but so does feces (it's true. All those dead cells have to leave the body somehow!) and so do tumors. Are we then to say that tumors are persons? Some of them have hair, teeth, even organs![1] Should the cells of Henrietta Lacks have to pay taxes and serve jury duty? It seems that being (a) human isn't enough to be a person.

But if an embryo is not a person, when does it become one? The legal answer, in most states, is the beginning of the second trimester. At about twelve weeks, that human thing formally called an embryo is now dubbed a fetus (from the Latin for "baby") and is now protected by federal and state laws, even though there is no physiological difference between a baby at 11 weeks, 6 days, 23 hours; and 12 weeks even— other than normal development (after all, every day during pregnancy a baby is more developed than the day before, and that trend continues in the child for the next twenty years). This arbitrary date seems to be when a human thing becomes a human person. Thus if an embryo is aborted on the last day of the first trimester, it's not murder because the embryo is not sufficiently developed to be a person. If a fetus is aborted on the first day of the second trimester, however, then it is a person's life which was taken and not just a collection of human cells inside someone's womb. I well understand the importance of arbitrary dates when legality is concerned. One cannot vote at the age of 17 years, 364 days; nor can one buy alcohol at 20 years, 365 days (leap year!). But perhaps that same tolerance of arbitrary dates is being used to decide whether killing is murder, or just the abortion of a lump that gives its mother weird cravings at two in the morning.

So why might the end-of-first-trimester deadline make sense? Beats me. I suppose it must be because embryos are less developed than fetūs. Though by that same logic, a four-year-old must be less of a person than a forty-year-old. Granted, children do have fewer privileges than adults, but have no less protection under the law. Child abuse is not looked upon with less scorn than abuse towards an adult, but then again that could be because children aren't persons so they can't defend themselves, so the penalty should be steeper. And children aren't persons so when they are tried for a crime, the court is more lenient. But if it were true that a child is less of a person, that would mean that murdering a child should be less heinous than murdering an adult. That must be true, what with all the popular support for the murder of a child named "Justin Bieber." So maybe it is true that the younger a child is, the less "person" it ought to be considered. That makes sense in terms of mass. So if an embryo only weighs an ounce, it just barely meets the mass requirements of being a person. Any less than that, and there's not enough human to make up a person. It's sort of like how, if you have one scoop of ice cream left in the freezer, you can't very well make a sundae, now can you? There's not enough ice cream there to be considered "sundae." But who decided how much human matter you should have before making person? The answer differs, it seems.

The most hard-core of proponents support late-term abortions, well into the third trimester. If I had to guess, I'd say that the majority of proponents shun these extremists as a little cuckoo and possibly spiteful, but prefer not to give extensive thought as to why they feel this shunning; for doing so would expose their hypocrisy. If you, dear reader, are yourself a proponent, I suppose right now you wish to stop reading so you can track me down and beat in my smug face, but I implore you to first let me defend my calling you a hypocrite. After that, anything is fair game. Why do I say moderate proponents are hypocritical when late-termers are not? It's very simple. Late-termers don't tolerate that arbitrary deadline which I referred to above. They don't have to wonder why a seven-week baby shouldn't be protected but an eight-week baby should. To them, as long as a human thingy is attached to its mother, it doesn't matter if the thing is undeveloped and weighs one pound, or if it has a full beard and weighs 100 pounds (ouch!)—it's still a non-person. With that being the case, we can only say that a human is a person once it is no longer attached to its mother. Meaning, when the umbilical cord is cut and not a second sooner. Before the umbilical cord is cut, the baby is still attached to its mother, and is therefore a part of her body. The only two differences after birth are that the baby now breathes oxygen through its throat, and it doesn't need protection (by the placenta) from being suspended in fluid. Other than that, nothing is different; it's still a part of her body. Is not a woman's hand a part of her body because it's attached via her wrist? Is not a woman's tooth a part of her body because it's cemented in gums? And would a woman's arm cease to be a part of her body were it severed in an accident?

With the wonders of modern technology it is possible to reattach a severed body part as long as the right conditions are met (time from severance, way in which part was severed, etc. are factors). Surgeons can replant various parts with reasonable success. With a transplant, immunosuppressant drugs are needed to prevent the host from attacking its guest, much in the same way your wife restrains you when you're enraged at her parasitic live-in brother. But when an arm is reattached to its own shoulder, instead of someone else's, no problems arise because the arm doesn't suddenly stop being a part of the body just because it was missing for a few minutes. Likewise, who's to say that a baby being severed from its mother after birth means it's no longer a part of her body? Imagine how much nicer teenagers would be to their mothers if the threat of abortion constantly loomed over their pimply heads. It's true that a child can't reenter its mother's vagina (unless that child's name is Oedipus—bow chicka wow wow!) but why squabble over physical impossibilities? A child inherits its mother's DNA and indeed, females inherit all of their mothers' mitochondrial DNA entirely, intact, generation after generation. Maybe that's why you're becoming more and more like her every year. If half of you owes its existence to her one ovum that didn't end up on a tampon, then according to the previous logic, doesn't that qualify you as literally, physically, a part of your mother's body? …I believe I have just made myself uncomfortable. Let us move on.

So if it's not okay to abort a child when it's four years old and won't stop singing the jingle from that annoying commercial, nor is it okay to abort a baby after it's born and before the umbilical cord is cut, why ought we to think it is acceptable or justifiable (more on that later) to abort a baby when it's still in the womb? Perhaps this is a case of "out of sight, out of mind." If you can't see a baby's hazel eyes, and its fingerprints, and you can't feel its beating heart, or let it wrap its tiny hand around your finger, then you won't have to think about ending its totally non-person life. Lest I rely entirely on pathos, however, and before I get too far ahead, I'd like to return to a previous paragraph in which I discussed the non-personhood of tumors and feces. In a spontaneous argument with a stranger on Facebook, I made the same argument as I did above, saying that an embryo is of course a person, because it has human DNA. My opponent the proponent responded with "This pre-med student isn't really sure where to start with that reasoning. Thanks for the laugh." She presumably referred to herself as "this pre-med student" to intimidate me, as if not yet being in med school were an awesome testament of her limitless medical knowledge. At least she was kind enough to thank me for making her laugh. After I further supported my argument, being sure to make liberal use of medical terms like "penis," she responded with the quote below.

" If you're arguing that cells with human DNA should be legally protected as people [sic], I hope you're consistent enough to have never masturbated and you're against the removal of cancerous tumors. If you think there is something different about fertilized eggs, being totipotent, and that they should be legally treated differently than [sic] other cells then say that but don't pretend that the systematic attempt to legitimize controlling women's bodies is all about "biology." "

Chuckles here is basing her reply on the misconception that I said individual cells other than zygotes are persons. While cells make up persons, they themselves are not (they don't have enough mass, remember?). Still, I do cherish all life and every time I poop, I mourn thirty days for the dead cells I just excreted. The difference between those cells and a zygote is, as she said, totipotency, which for you non-Latin speakers, means "capable of the whole." That part of her response was right on the money. No cell in the body will split into two, then four, then eight, and so on; nor will it grow a few heart cells and a few lung cells until it has its own organs and an umbilical cord. Because of that same inactivity, an ovum is not a person until it is fertilized. Were it otherwise, a woman would bleed out thousands of living persons in her lifetime. A man would lose billions more. Luckily God is not so harsh in his dealings with our mortal race. Aside from miscarriages, a baby will only die if it's killed before even having a chance to screw up its life like the rest of us. By the way, if you're wondering why I keep referring to an embryo as "it," there are two reasons: "it" is easier to write than (s)he every single time, and an embryo's gender is indiscernible visually until the 8th week. Up until then the baby develops both sets of sex organs, meaning that every male has a uterus. Pretty cool, huh?

Up until the end of her response I was unwavering. But then, the last line caused an epiphany. Here it is again. "…don't pretend that the systematic attempt to legitimize controlling women's bodies is all about "biology." " That line hit me like Ron Artest's fists at a Pistons game. How could I be such a sexist my whole life? Here I was, trying to control women like an issue of *Cosmo*! But now that I have seen the light, I shall resolve to let women, and especially pregnant women, exercise the rights that God and probably George Washington intended them to have! If a pregnant woman wants to smoke, or drink, then by Jove, take her down to 7-11! It's her body, and it's her choice! If she wants to get drunk to celebrate finally being able to conceive with the help of doctors and a Petri dish, then that's her God-given right! What's that, you say? Alcohol causes Fetal Alcohol Syndrome? You say that the decision to drink will affect her baby? Well, the last time I checked, abortion also affects the baby. How is it that one could think nothing of damage done to an embryo as long as it's fatal, but recoil in horror at the thought of damage that results in deformity but not death?

There's the real question there. To understand the thinking behind your typical abortion, we must understand the events that usually precede it. Every year, nearly 1.2 million women in the U.S. have an abortion. The most common reasons are inability to support a child, to end an unwanted pregnancy, to spare a child its congenital deformities, conception by rape or incest, or a condition that endangers the life of the mother and/or the child. About 30% of abortions come from teenage mothers. Rather than express my moral outrage at teenagers having sex or some other such thing, I will express sympathy for every mother who feels abortion is the best option. It's truly sad when circumstances drive a mother to choose such an awful selection. Never let it be said that I can't speak credibly about this issue because I have a Y chromosome (my father's sperm's choice, not mine) or that I can't understand what these mothers are going through because I'm incapable of being pregnant. I have a uterus too, you know!

Hollywood must have quite an impact on our way of thinking when we feel it justifiable to kill a child in order to put a Quasimodo out of the misery we assume he'll suffer in life because of his defects. Because if there's one thing movies have taught us, it's that only the beautiful can be happy. And do we really think that it is better to kill a child than to spare it a life of suffering? Are you kidding me? What human doesn't suffer? Shouldn't we all be dead right now? We cannot know the destiny of our children, but God knows what difference they could make. Frederick Douglass was raised in cruel slavery and used his awful history to further abolition. If he could make beauty of tragedy, who's to say some other child born into poverty or malady could not? Really, all of these circumstances are merely excuses, sought out to end a burden on the mother/parents—except for the last, of course. If a mother has to choose between her baby's death and both of their deaths, I hope she'll choose the former. It's better that the baby should die when its fate is already sealed, than for both of them to die needlessly.

But as tragic or excruciating as a situation may be, I cannot think of a single situation in which murder becomes justifiable. Not wanting a baby is hardly a convincing reason. If you eat doughnuts, you have no right to complain about your twelve chins. And if you have sex, don't complain about pregnancy. I'm talking to you too, scared boyfriend. In the Saudi peninsula and elsewhere before the 7th century, it was not uncommon for impoverished parents to leave newborn girls in the desert to die, because a strong, be-muscled son can help with farm work but a girl would be just another mouth to feed. This is why the Qur'an contains a verse, XVII:31, encouraging couples to bear through tough times and have faith that they will be provided for. The Bible also contains multiple verses (Deuteronomy 12:30-31, 18:10, etc.) forbidding any kind of infanticide (that word sounds a lot dirtier than "abortion," doesn't it?), so either the Hebrews also practiced infanticide, or God had the foresight to address others (He's a pretty smart guy, you know). I said all that to say this: there is a long and ignoble history of struggling parents who felt incapable of caring for a child. But no one is alone. There's a lot to be said for humbly asking friends/family for assistance, or even resorting to adoption. Adoption is a good choice! Nobody who doesn't want kids is going to adopt them.

"But John," you say, because apparently you don't know this is a one-way conversation, "What about pregnancy by rape? Surely you don't expect a poor girl to care for a baby that was violently forced upon her! Don't you think abortion in this case would be best?" No, I don't. I said before that I can't think of any situation that would justify murder, and I meant it. I agree that rape is a horrible thing and being pregnant by rape is awful, but why punish the baby for the crime? Why not abort the rapist? I am obviously not being serious, but if you are willing to take a life for a rape-pregnancy, why not make it the man who caused it? If you are in support of abortion, you're almost definitely liberal when it comes to other issues as well. What's my point? Well, with that being the case, you are against capital punishment. Remember when I called you a hypocrite before? Yeah, I meant that too. How could anyone disapprove of sentencing to death a (wo)man who took another life (possibly several lives) and yet throw support behind killing a baby whose only crime is existing, and against its own will? I assure you, no one on Earth was consulted before being conceived. Existing is not anyone's choice.

And just before you say I'm not aware of the thing I'm about to elaborate on, "out-of-sight, out-of-mind" morality can be found in other areas of our lives, as well. It's easy to enjoy how cheap chocolate is when it comes from child slaves in West Africa. It's easy to enjoy the affordability of electronics that were assembled by quasi-slaves in China after the raw materials were sent there from child slaves in central Africa, and it's easy to enjoy our pristine cars when we don't have to consider the high rate of carjackers in South Africa. We all turn a blind eye–and we shouldn't–but if you are able to stop a death, don't you think you should?

Of course, there is a reason this debate continues to rage on. The reason is that persons (especially those in a rich society like ours) have a bafflingly strong sense of entitlement. They want what they want, and they believe whatever is convenient to them. That is why many persons believe the 1969 Moon landing was a hoax, despite there being *freaking footprints on the lunar surface*! There are those who believe 9/11 was an inside job, that President Obama was not born in Hawai'i, and that the Holocaust, an event which left behind many survivors *who were there at the time*, never happened. We believe what we want to, despite minor considerations like "facts" and "logic." It's a concept Stephen Colbert referred to as "truthiness." Why think with your head when you can feel with your gut? If you want to believe embryos aren't persons, you will, never mind facts and logic.

So do I think that women who have abortions because their boyfriends impregnated them and then refused to support the children are bad persons? Well, that question isn't fair, because I think everyone is a bad person, including myself. (Remember that sense of entitlement? We shouldn't call ourselves good if we've done bad things.) What I am saying is that, despite the crappy hand that some of us were dealt, and despite being burdened with a commitment of 18 years and ~$200,000, two wrongs never make a right. And if you choose to push forward despite that massive burden, despite that unprecedented disruption in your life, and despite having to do it without the support of that idiot who knocked you up, then what will that perseverance say of your character? When you refuse to take the easy way out because you consider even one death of a tiny person that doesn't even have a name yet inexcusable, what will that say of your courage? And when you didn't beat me up for calling you a hypocrite, how much money did you save on not driving all the way to my house? Fight. Fight, and never surrender.

Finished April 2011

P.S. Two points I didn't bring up in the article proper are the proponents' argument that embryos can't live without their mothers, and the fact that premature babies can be sustained in an incubator. The first argument is used by proponents to say that embryos aren't persons because if they were removed from the care of mommy, they would die. I would like to point out to these eagle-eyed geniuses that newborn babies also cannot survive without their mothers for lack of milk, and most urbanites would probably die if the supply trucks stopped filling the shelves at the grocery store. As for the second point, if babies are born far too early, say at 23 weeks, there is a good chance they will survive in an incubator until it's safe to live in room temperature like the other babies. My point to this is, what if technology reached the point to where a test tube baby didn't need human gestation at all? What then, would we say of its personhood, when it shares the same situation as comatose patients? Oh yeah, and the umbilical cord doesn't even attach to the mother until week five, so before that, an abortion wouldn't be doing anything to the mother's body. It's the embryo's body, so it should be the embryo's choice. I am strongly pro-choice!

1. Kuno N, Kadomatsu K, Nakamura M, Miwa-Fukuchi T, Hirabayashi N, Ishizuka T (January 2004). "Mature ovarian cystic teratoma with a highly differentiated homunculus: a case

report". *Birth Defects Research. Part a, Clinical and Molecular Teratology* **70** (1): 40–6.

Bonus article! The libertarian gets mad at YouTube and copyright law! Let's have a bit of a giggle innit!

"I am Copyright Claim! Look on my works, ye mighty, and despair."

This image is a joke. Just keep reading.

By now I'm sure you've at least heard about copyright claims wreaking havoc across YouTube. If you haven't, many videos should give you an eye and earful. Content ID has been around since 2009, but last year something strange happened. It was as if Google, feeling scorned by the world's rejection of its precious baby Google+, went crazy-psycho and loosed its dog on YouTube, quickly killing off several channels whose videos were protected under the "Fair Use" clause of US copyright law.

But don't worry, there's no way this will ruin YouTube. Content creators aren't going to flock to other sites since YouTube gets 20 times the traffic as its nearest competitor. The money to be earned from AdSense is greater than that from any other video site. So here we are stuck in this limbo while an over-eager system classifies videos as being infringements, even when the uploaders have companies' permission to use them. Many companies such as Valve and Facepunch Studios encourage let's play videos and machinima, knowing that communities are eager to show their love and that they can produce videos that are essentially free advertising, only to have Content ID automatically tag these videos as infringing. This happens even to original content creators.

Valve in particular has shown time and time again that not using copyright law to stifle innovation will benefit everyone. Compare the stories of the *Chrono Trigger* fan remake and the *Half-Life* fan remake named *Black Mesa*. When *CT* owner Square Enix got wind of the remake's development, they issued a cease and desist, ending their fans' work on what looked to be a very promising love letter to one of the SNES' best games. Square Enix has yet to develop their own remake even nine years later. When Valve got wind of *Black Mesa*, on the other hand, they shrugged and went about their business. Ten years later, *Black Mesa* is nearing a Steam release after being greenlighted by the community and when it finally does hit Steam, Valve will collect a standard platform fee of 30% for each sale. They didn't have to lift a finger to make this game, and they'll collect tens of thousands of dollars off of it. That is how you copyright, ladies and gentlemen.

Of course, videos are no longer automatically deleted (as they are on Dailymotion.com and other sites) but they are tagged as belonging to the copyright holder. The video is then blocked from viewing in certain countries (based on certain factors) until the uploader acknowledges the claim. When this happens the claimant (called the "third party") will receive ad revenue from the video, even if it's a so-called "transformative work" put together by the uploader. What this means is that a publisher (Viacom, Zenimax, FOX, etc.) needs only to claim copyright of a particular work and YouTube users will be forced to acknowledge this ownership whether it's valid or not. Here's a perfect example. Last year I uploaded an **unlisted** video to YouTube of students playing "Twinkle, Twinkle, Little Star" for **non-commercial** purposes. Everything was fine and dandy for a few months, but suddenly I lost my ability to upload videos over 15 minutes long! I had been uploading several gameplay videos, most recently the one of *Super Mario Bros.*, but just as soon as they were up I acknowledged the copyright and no longer had any violations–or so I thought. Scrolling down to check every one of my videos, I noticed that new claims all of a sudden popped up against my violin videos. And one of them was for "Twinkle, Twinkle, Little Star."

In case you don't know the history of that particular song, let me break it down. "Twinkle" originated with a French melody called "Ah! Vous dirai-je, Maman" which was published in 1761. It was arranged in a theme-and-variation (K 265/300e) by Mozart in 1780, and set to words in a poem called "The Star" by Jane Taylor in 1806. So without copyright law, we have a collaboration of sorts between a French dude, an Austrian guy, and an English lady across five decades. You'll notice that all of these dates are from a really long time ago, and US law grants copyright to an author for 70 years after his/her death. And I was forced to acknowledge that it belonged to "multiple third-party claimants" in order for my video not to be blocked.

The Stupid, It Burns

Even after giving into their demands, my account still didn't grant me the ability to upload videos over fifteen minutes in length, hence the need for my second YouTube channel. Also, I decided it would be a good idea to make an account with DailyMotion.com as a back-up. This took a bit more work than you might think; I neglected to save back-up copies on my hard drive so I had to extract those first.

But now I won't have to worry about my videos disappearing since I have two back-ups and now I get to upload long videos. What's the downside, you might ask? Well, now that YouTube accounts are tied to Google+ and so is Blogger, I have to use a different browser to upload videos for that account or else I'll have to sign in-and-out in order to work with my blog and videos. And all of this could have been avoided by publishers not claiming to own a song that's been in the public domain for two hundred years.

So what's the moral? What can you take away from this? Simply: If someone wants to do something cool with your idea, let 'im. If his product is better than yours, you'll either be forced to improve your own, or you can use his product's lower quality to advertise your own (much in the same way that commercials refer to their products being better than the "leading brand"). Maybe that's why companies are so eager to suppress derivative works–they don't want to compete by making better ideas.

Anyway, my blog is copyrighted, but I'd rather that someone rip off my ideas than to continue having my ideas be unknown. But maybe that's just me. Anyway, if you want to use The King of Martian Cats in your stories or paintings, go ahead.

www.ingramcontent.com/pod-product-compliance
Lightning Source LLC
Chambersburg PA
CBHW062018280526
45787CB00005B/2146